# WILTSHIRE

*of one hundred years ago*

SHANE'S CASTLE, DEVIZES

RAISING STONES AT AVEBURY

# WILTSHIRE

*of one hundred years ago*

# DAVID BUXTON

ALAN SUTTON

First published in the United Kingdom in 1991 by
Alan Sutton Publishing Litd · Phoenix Mill · Stroud · Gloucestershire

First published in the United States of America in 1992 by
Alan Sutton Publishing Inc · Wolfeboro Falls · NH 03896–0848

British Library Cataloguing in Publication Data

Buxton, David, 1944–
Wiltshire of one hundred years ago.
I. Title
942.319

ISBN 0–7509–0031–8

Library of Congress Cataloguing in Publication Data applied for

CORSHAM

Endpapers, Front: J. Lott and Sons, Regent Street, Swindon; *WL*. Back: Taylor's fairground engine, *Victoria*, 1910; *Jennings family*.

Typeset in 11/13 Bembo.
Typesetting and origination by
Alan Sutton Publishing Limited.
Printed in Great Britain by
The Bath Press Limited.

# Preface

The aim of this book, *Wiltshire of One Hundred Years Ago* is to recreate some of the flavour of life in a period of the county's history that is only just outside living memory. By using a wealth of carefully chosen and well-reproduced photographs of the period and placing them alongside extracts from good descriptive writing of those years I hope to give the reader an insight into some of the life and times of the working people of the late nineteenth century and early twentieth century in Wiltshire and at the same time make the journey an enjoyable one.

I have for as long as I can remember been fascinated by old photographs. That in a part of a second a whole scene can be fixed and held indefinitely for later study still seems incredible. There is so much to see in these photographs. Just look at some of the faces in this book, peering sometimes with obvious distrust, sometimes with open amusement, at the camera. Sometimes caught without their knowledge. We notice styles of dress, the simple hard-wearing and often much-mended working clothes of the farm labourer and the elaborate, bulky formality of

dresses worn by women going to church or the Jubilee celebrations. We can note the difference between town and country formal wear but also the similarity of working clothes worn by the farm and factory workers. We notice immediately the wide, often empty streets because we are accustomed to seeing streets full of motor cars. We may look wistfully at pretty thatched cottages and their occupants fitting our romantic image of old rural life but we must not be fooled by appearances. These cottages were cold and damp in winter, they lacked power and sanitation and were usually crowded. The inhabitants were poor and could rarely afford good food or domestic comforts. A far cry from the modernized cottages of today in which it is possible to be comfortable and still pretend to be following a rural lifestyle.

Most of the photographs and texts chosen for the book date from the 1880s to just after the turn of the century and although some stray a few years outside these limits I have included these as well because I believe they are typical of that late nineteenth-century period and because they help

MARKET LAVINGTON

MINETY

to produce a balance to the overall picture. I have not attempted to include every town and village in the county although the spread is geographically wide and fairly representative of the regional agricultural areas too, namely the grassy downlands (the *chalk*) and the arable and dairying areas (the *cheese*). Inevitably, for such a rural county, farming life is well represented but life in the market town is here too and by sharp contrast so are scenes of industry in the north of the county represented by Swindon and particularly the railway factories of the GWR.

The photographs I have chosen come from a large number available from this period taken mainly by the professional photographers who proliferated in even the smallest towns by the 1870s. The record that they left is a tribute to their impressive activities in recording as picture postcards even the smallest and most remote villages and hamlets.

We are fortunate also to have a good choice of country writers for this period. Wiltshire was home to some of the most perceptive and eloquent commentators on country life that this nation has seen. Richard Jefferies, W.H. Hudson and Alfred Williams all wrote with sympathy and understanding and sometimes with anger of the plight of the labouring classes and some of the best examples of their work are used here. The experiences of Williams on farms and in factories gave him a unique insight into the state of rural and industrial workers of the time. Although life was hard, there were moments of fun and laughter; for the Swindon works, Trip Day was the highlight of the

year and for the farm labourer, the Harvest Home was a chance to be merry at the farmer's expense and for everyone there was always a trip to the fair to look forward to.

The assembling of the material for this book gave me a great deal of fun and satisfaction and I hope that the result will give as much pleasure to others. In producing the book I have received help from a large number of people who have loaned their pictures and books to me and offered advice and comment on all aspects of the research. I would like to thank: Alan Alexander, Jean Allen, J. Backhouse, Dennis Bird, Trustees of the Bowood Collection, Fred Chivers, Gwen Chivers, Pamela Coleman, CPRE, Robert Dickenson, Jack Field, Kate Fielden, Marion Fryer, Felicity Gilmour, Michael Grey, Peggy Gye, Lionel Hailstone, Lorna Hayock, Danny Howell, the Jennings Family, Richard Larden, Michael Marshman, Alec Moulding, Robert Newman, Philip Oram, Michael Palmer, Derek Parker, Roger Pope, Rex Sawyer, The Swindon Society, Megan Williams, Wiltshire Life Society, Tim and Helen Withers and the Staffs of Wiltshire Library and Museum Service, Salisbury and South Wilts Museum, Warminster Museum, Swindon Museum and Art Gallery, Devizes Museum and the Fox Talbot Museum at Lacock. Last but not least I want to thank my own family, Sue, Rupert and Tom for their undying help and patience whilst I was compiling this book.

David Buxton
Devizes
Wiltshire

# Introduction

The Wiltshire landscape is a striking one dominated by great expanses of chalk downland which spread from Salisbury Plain in the south to the Marlborough Downs in the north. This was traditionally an area of sheep and corn farming. The sheep were fed on the rolling downs by day and folded in sheep hurdles at night to manure the land for the crops that were to follow. On the lower lying, clay vales dairy cattle have for centuries produced the milk for cheese and butter. The downlands were areas of large estates and small, compact and often isolated villages. The manorial system of the Middle Ages with a communal agricultural system and peasant farmer survived in Wiltshire in a recognisable form right up to the nineteenth century. But much earlier than this, Wiltshire was home to some of the first farming communities in northern Europe and if we are to judge by the amount of evidence that survives from those prehistoric times it must have been a very important settlement area. The country abounds with burial mounds, circles and earthworks of all kinds, proof of centuries of activity, both agricultural and ritual by these early inhabitants. Some of the monuments that they left are still so impressive that they are among the best known and most visited sites in the world. The great stone circles of Avebury and Stonehenge attract between them, about one million visitors each year.

Farming still represents the principle economic activity of Wiltshire but from the earliest times to the nineteenth century there had been little real change in the way the land was used and the way the people were employed on it. From around the middle of the last century however, a series of major events took place that were to change the lot of the farmer and labourer alike and the role of agriculture in the economy of the area.

The Wiltshire farm labourer had always been poor and yet had been worked very hard by his masters. The landowners and farmers had traditionally taken advantage of a poor and submissive work force who had largely accepted their poor lot and put up with conditions that were often appalling. Even in the mid-nineteenth century when their industrial counterparts were beginning to become more organised and to demand better pay and conditions, agricultural workers remained largely quiescent and politicaly apathetic, even when increasing mechanisation on the farms began to reduce the number of jobs. The nature of their work meant that they were isolated in small villages and often ignorant of developments in nearby towns. The only serious agricultural revolts of the century had occured in the 1830s, one of which had involved the so called Tolpuddle Martyrs in Dorset, and these had been heavily put down, ending in hangings and transportation. It was not until the end of the century that farm labourers in the south began to see any real improvements in their working conditions. But by this time the farmers and landowners were themselves in severe difficulties.

STEAM THRESHING AT RUTLANDS FARM

Farming in the area witnessed a serious depression which began towards the end of the 1870s and from which it did not fully recover until 1914. Rapidly declining prices for farm produce caused a great many farmers to go out of business and subsequently put many labourers out of work. The competition from abroad, particularly cheap wheat from North America that poured in following the repeal of the Corn Laws, coincided with a series of bad harvests. Cold, wet summers were the main cause which culminated in the disastrous harvest of 1879. The price of corn fell dramatically. In 1847 wheat had sold for 70 shillings a quarter but by 1870 foreign competition had caused a fall to 46 shillings and by 1894 the price was down to 24 shillings. Sheep and dairy cattle were also badly affected by the wet, cold weather and large losses resulted through disease and a shortage of hay for winter feed. Such a decline in the fortunes of the main industry of the county meant more hardship for the farm labourer than even he had experienced in the past. Richard Jefferies in his books of this period describes many examples of the sorry state of the farmers and labourers at this time. Brought up on a small farm at Coate near Swindon he witnessed his father's own financial decline and wrote with eloquence and obvious bitterness about farm closures and the pain felt by struggling farmers at the time. An extract from his essay *Sold by Auction* is included in this book (p.63) which describes a farmer looking on as his farm is split up and sold around him.

Although Jefferies has been criticised for his attitudes to the farm labourer, which appear at times to be unfair it should be remembered that he wrote from the point of view of the small farmer and although at times he is cynical of the labourer at other times he shows a deep respect and pays tribute to his hardworking loyalty. There are examples in this book which show this and there are other examples too which demonstrate his strong love of the Wiltshire countryside. Whilst he undoubtedly understood the need for farm development and progress he also shows his nostalgic feelings for the 'old ways' (p.20) when he laments the declining need for the farm horse in the face of steam power.

So what did the unemployed and destitute do when farm work was no longer available? If they were old or sick they would probably have ended up in the most infamous of Victorian institutions, the union workhouse. The workhouse replaced parish relief and parish poor-houses in 1834. Parish relief was administered by the Overseers of the Poor, unpaid parish officials who distributed what small amounts they had available for residents of the parish. Under the new system parishes were gathered together into 'Unions' and relief was only provided in the workhouse, where conditions were deliberately made unattractive in order to discourage applications for help. The workhouses were loathed by the poor and understandably so. The regime in a workhouse was such that although food, clothes and a bed were provided the atmosphere was that of a prison rather than a home. The attendants were often harsh towards the inmates and ran the daily routine to a cruel set of rules. Elderly married couples were separated on arrival to live apart in different wings of the same building for the rest of their lives. The workhouse system survived well into the present century and although the regime became less harsh with time the loathing for them persisted. I heard a first hand account from an old lady in Devizes who recalled an experience at the local workhouse when a child. She accompanied her mother to visit an old lady resident who was known to them. The old lady was thirsty and asked for a drink of

GWR WORKS, SWINDON

water but when the young girl obtained one and was passing it to her, an attendant angrily knocked it from her hand causing it to spill on the floor, because she said it was not yet time to give the inmates a drink.

The middle class Victorian attitude to poverty was a curious mixture of compassion and harshness and often it seemed to treat poverty as though it were a crime itself. The response to poaching illustrates this well. The poaching of game from a big estate in Wiltshire by a poor man with a hungry family must have been to him an easily justifiable act but the force with which the landlord protected the game for his own sport was impressive and the law gave full weight to the protection he sought. Well armed game keepers hunted poachers like they hunted weasels or jays and poachers were often shot dead. If captured they faced severe punishments. Richard Jefferies wrote a cynical essay called *Shooting Poachers* (p.112) that gives vent to his angry disapproval of this approach and an account by W.H. Hudson, *Deer Stealers* (p.87) illustrates the wrath of the Wiltshire gamekeeper. Poor country people stole for other kinds of basic needs too, contemporary newspapers are full of court proceedings in which severe, unsympathetic punishments are handed out for stealing bread, garden produce and clothes (p.102).

The able-bodied farm worker who became unemployed in the 1880s and 1890s may have sought work abroad, it was a time for emigration to the New World but more likely he would have moved to the local town to seek work. In Wiltshire this was often to the north and Swindon, which was rapidly becoming a major industrial centre. The GWR (Great Western Railway) manufactured almost all that was required to operate a major railway company in one huge works and this was where many went. Men who had grown up ploughing fields and tending sheep learned to operate machines in conditions of heat and dirt that were unimaginable on a farm. The pay was not good but it was better than they had been used to. We know a good deal about what it was like to make this cultural move to Swindon through the eyes of Alfred Williams. Having left the fields to work as a hammerman in the forge-sheds of the GWR works himself, he wrote about his experiences in *Life in a Railway factory*. This famous account not only describes in detail each part and process of the factory but it is also an important social document of all aspects of life in a factory of this time. Williams was an articulate, self-educated man who spoke out against oppression and the poor treatment of factory workers and because he had already acquired a national reputation for his writing ('The Hammerman Poet') his words could not be ignored. Later he left the factories to

SWINDON

return to his rural home and wrote *A Wiltshire Village* from which we may learn in great detail the ways of the Wiltshire village at the turn of the century and earlier. Like Jefferies he loved the Wiltshire landscape and it's people and some of his descriptions of both are delightful. One envies him his pleasure at following the horse drawn reaper in a cornfield:

What a delicious smell there is in the wake of the reaping machine too! The hay field is sweet, but the harvest field is far sweeter, just after the corn is cut; it is very balm, the quintessence of delightful odours and perfumes, rich and sensuous. The straw itself is fragrant.

And enjoy his poetic description of the steam-threshing machine at work:

It was wonderful for them to see the black smoke towering out of the tall iron chimney, the piston rod shooting silently in and out, the wheels spinning round and the long conveyor belt communicating power to the thresher, the chaff and chaving flying, and the straw rustling down behind. The humming of the thresher has a peculiar fascination as well, especially at that time of year; it sounds mournful and plaintive borne to you over the field; it is like a dirge to the dying year, yet it is not a depressing sound at all, but exactly fits in with the surroundings of the farm and countryside.

To add to this 'pictorial' descriptive writing we have of course, a very good pictorial record in the photographs taken by the many professional and amateur photographers of the period. This was in many ways a heyday of photography. The photographic process had been invented and patented in the late 1840s by a Wiltshireman, Henry Fox Talbot at his home in Lacock, by the 1860s it

COLIN CHIVERS, DEVIZES

was already a technique available to the masses. Professional and photographic studios opened in every town and many individuals took up photography as a hobby. Portrait photographs became commonplace and photographers added to their income by photographing local scenes and also local events. These could be celebrations such as jubilees, the unveiling of a new statue (p.18) or a local disaster such as a house fire or a tramcar accident. Newspapers were not illustrated until after the turn of the century and local photographers often found a ready sale for such pictures. Some photographers specialised in novelty effects such as Mr Hooper in Swindon who invented a device to photograph flashes of lightning. Hooper also began a series of record photograhs of places described in the books of Richard Jefferies. One of these was of Job Brown's cottage (p.17). John Chivers of Devizes took a series of portraits of children in costume. There is a print taken by him of an elaborately posed replica of the famous 'Bubbles' painting by Millais and on this page is his son dressed as a cowboy.

It was in the late 1890s that the picture postcard was introduced and immediately became popular. Postcards were sent in huge numbers all the year round to communicate short messages to friends. They seem to have served much the same purpose that a telephone message does today. To supply this demand local photographers took pictures of even the smallest villages, happily many of these have survived to provide material not only for the collector and the local historian but also for this glimpse of *Wiltshire of one hundred years ago.*

MR HOOPER THE PHOTOGRAPHER, SWINDON

# WILTSHIRE

*of one hundred years ago*

# CHARLES SLOPER & SON, DEVIZES.

## NURSERY CHAIRS.

6/11

4 6 4/11
6/11 8/11

5/11 6/11 7/11
8/11 10/11 12/11

5/11 6/11

12 6 13 6 14/11
15/11 19/11 22/6
with pan, 15/11

4 11 5/6
low chair
4/6

5 11 6/11
low chair
4/6

**UPHOLSTERED
SINGLE CARS.**
Two positions, carved
satin walnut, 35/6,
39/6, 45/-, 55 -, 3/3/-,
and upwards.

**WHITE CANE
CARS.**
Single, various designs,
two positions,
42/-, 3/3/-, 3/12 6, 4/1 -,
5/5/-.

**BENT SIDES,
COACH FINISH.**
3/3/-, 3/15/-, 4/4/-

**UPHOLSTERED
DOUBLE CARS.**
For one or two children.
Various designs.
42/-, 45/-, 47/6, 49/6,
52/6.

**DOUBLE OR SINGLE
CANE CARS.**
3/3/-, 4/4/-, 4/17/6.

## HAVE YOU GOT A SAFETY COT NET?

2ft. × 4ft.
Iron Cot. 15/11.
Strong ditto, 17/11.

2ft. × 4ft.
Brass Rail Cot, 22 6.
Superior Ditto, 27 6,
and upwards.

Other sizes to order.

2ft. × 4ft.
Iron Cot with drop sides, 22 6.
Brass Rail ditto ditto, 35/9.
Ditto with spring bed 2/2/-
(as shown),

## We have always AN ASSORTMENT OF CHILDREN'S STRONG TOYS in Stock.

**TRICYCLE HORSES.**
27/6 30/- 32/6

**SAFETY ROCKING HORSES.**
21/- 24 6 29 6 42/- 59/6

**ROCKING HORSES.**
12 11 21/- 28/6 39/6

**TOY PERAMBULATORS.**
Rubber tyred wheels
Brass jointed hoods
15/11 19/11 21/-

A GOOD TOY CREATES JOY IN THE NURSERY.

MARSTON

## MOWING

For several days old Jemmy had been preparing the 'sheen,' cleaning and oiling the parts, sharpening the knives, and getting everything ready to begin the mowing. He had his headquarters in the cart-house; there he filed and filed, and hammered and tinkered till all was in perfect order. The special harness for the mares was cleaned and oiled; he made a cushion for himself, to fix on the seat, out of a sack stuffed with hay; his long whip was ready; he used cords for reins. When the tops of the grasses were turning ripe and the weather was settling down fine, Launcelot gave the word. Jemmy coupled up the two young mares and set out for the field. They were very frightened and restless at first with the rattle of the machine; Jemmy tugged the reins, struck them sharply with the whip, and scolded them soundly with 'Now then-a,' and 'Wai then,' and 'Stand still, oot.' They pawed about, then started forward, then ran back, now wheeled round, till at last they came to understand what was required. Then, nodding their heads quickly, one against the other, they half ran toward the gate leading to the meadow, nearly shaking Jemmy from the seat. So he set about the first field, going round, and round, and round the piece, sometimes halting a moment to clear the cut grass from the knife at an angle, and take a wet of ale from the bottle; then on again, with jacket and waistcoat thrown aside, and broad-brimmed felt hat; now flicking the horses with the whip, or gripping the lever which raised the knife in passing over a trench or gutter. The machine tinkled merrily; the flanks of the mares became white with the foam of the perspiration; the sun shone hotter and hotter. About nine o'clock Jemmy stopped for lunch – a mouthful of bread and cheese, and a long pull at the bottle. This time the mares were allowed to eat their lunch, too; a pile of the sweet juicy grass was set before them, and the iron bit was removed from the mouth. Now Launcelot came strolling up, paddle in hand, and sometimes turned a swath over with it, and soon departed again. Half an hour before noon Jemmy released the mares from the machine, and took them away to the farm for water and a rest till the evening; then back to the field and on again. You could hear the tinkle of the machine till late twilight; then he came down to the farm, had his supper in the brew-house – bread, cheese, lettuce, young onions, and abundant ale; then off home to bed

*Alfred Williams*

HOME FARM, BOWOOD

## FARM CHILDREN

In the coldest weather one or more of the labourer's children are sure to be found in the farmyard somewhere. After the mother has dressed her boy (who may be about three or four years old) in the morning, he is at once turned out of doors to take care of himself, and if, as is often the case, the cottage is within a short distance of the farmyard, thither he toddles directly. He stands about the stable door, watching the harnessing of the great cart-horses, which are, from the very first, the object of his intense admiration. But he has already learnt to keep out of the way, knowing that his presence would not otherwise be tolerated a moment, and occupies a position which enables him to dart quickly behind a tree, or a rick.

When the horses are gone he visits the outhouse, where the steam-engine is driving the chaff-cutter, or peers in at the huge doors of the barn, where with wide wooden shovel the grain is being moved. Or he may be met with round the hay-ricks, dragging a log of wood by a piece of tar cord, the log representing a plough. As you come upon him suddenly he draws up to the rick as if the hay was his natural protector, and looks up at you with half-frightened, half-curious gaze, and mouth open. His hat is an old one of his father's, a mile too big, coming down over his ears to his shoulders, well greased from ancient use – a thing not without its advantage, since it makes it impervious to rain. He wears what was a white jacket, but

is now the colour of the prevailing soil of the place; a belt; and a pair of stumping boots, the very picture in miniature of his father's, heeled and tipped with iron. His naked legs are red with the cold, but thick and strong; his cheeks are plump and firm, his round blue eyes bright, his hair almost white, like bleached straw.

An hour or two ago his skin was clean enough, for he was sent out well washed, but it is now pretty well grimed, for he has been making himself happy in the dirt, as a boy should do if he be a boy. for one thing it is clean dirt, nothing but pure mother earth, and not the nasty unctuous filth of city courts and back lanes. If you speak to him he answers you sturdily – if you can catch the meaning of his words, doubly difficult from accent and imperfect knowledge of construction. But he means well, and if you send him on an errand will run off to find 'measter' as fast as his short stature will allow. He will potter about the farmyard the whole morning, perhaps turning up at home for a lunch of a slice of bread well larded. His little sister, not so old as himself, is there, already beginning her education in the cares of maternity, looking after the helpless baby that crawls over the wooden threshold of the door with bare head, despite the bitter cold. Once during the day he may perhaps steal round the farmhouse, and peer wistfully from behind the tubs or buckets into the kitchen, when, if the mistress chances to be about, he is pretty certain to pick up some trifle in the edible line.

. PEWSEY

How those prosperous parents who dwell in highly-rented suburban villas, and send out their children for a walk with a couple of nurses and a 'bow-wow' to run beside the perambulator, would be eaten up with anxiety did their well-dressed boys or girls play where this young son of toil finds his amusement! Under the very hoofs of the cart-horses – he will go out to them when they are loose in the field, three or four in a group, under a tree, when it looks as if the slightest movement on their part must crush him; down to the side of the deep broad brook to swim sticks in it for boats, where a slip on the treacherous mud would plunge him in, and where the chance of rescue – everybody being half a mile away at work – would be absolutely *nil*. The cows come trampling through the yard; the bull bellows in the meadow; great, grunting sows, savage when they have young, go by, thrusting their noses into and turning up the earth for food; steam ploughing engines pant and rumble about; carts are continually coming and going; and he is all day in the midst of it without guardian of any kind whatsoever. The fog, and frost, and cutting winter winds make him snivel and cry with the cold, and yet there he is out in it – in the draughts that blow round the ricks, and through the hedge bare of leaves. The rain rushes down pitilessly – he creeps inside the barn or shed, and with a stick splashes the puddles. The long glaring days of summer see him exposed to the scorching heat in the hay, or the still hotter harvest field. Through it all he grows stout and strong, and seems happy enough.

He is, perhaps, more fortunate than his sister, who has

BRATTON

ENFORD

ISAAC HABGOOD, BOWERCHALKE

to take part in the household work from very early age. But the village school claims them both after awhile; and the greater number of such schools are well filled, taking into consideration the long distances the children have to come and the frequent bad state of the roads and lanes. Both the employers and the children's own parents get them to school as much as possible; the former put on a mild compulsion, the latter for the most part are really anxious for the schooling, and have even an exaggerated idea of the value of education. In some cases it would seem as if the parents actually educated themselves in some degree from their own children, questioning them as to what they have been told. But, on the other hand, the labourer objects to paying for the teaching, and thinks the few coppers he is charged a terrible extortion.

*Richard Jefferies*

## LITTLE JACK PINNEGER

'Thomas,' said Mistress Large to her loving spouse, 'do 'e go into the garden and cut us a cabbage. We've got the pot on to-day.'

Master Large stood not on the order of his going, but trudged off at once to the kitchen-garden without saying a word. Having selected two or three of the finest cabbages, he drew forth his clasp-knife, and was about to sever them from their stalks, when the voice of a boy arrested his

EASTERTON

attention, and suspended the operation.

'Maester,' said the child, 'wull 'e let m' chainge hats wi' thuck galley-crow yander?'

The worthy farmer looked up, and saw the boy pointing to a scare-crow at the other end of the garden.

'Who bist thee?' he inquired.

The boy stared stupidly, and blushed until his sun-burnt and freckled face looked several shades darker.

'What's thee name, mun?' said the farmer.

'Pinneger, maester,' replied the boy.

'Pinneger! What, bist thee a Pinneger? How many's thee mother got at whome?' –

'Zeven, maester.'

'Zeven!' –

'Eez.'

'Massey upon us!' exclaimed the farmer, compassionately; 'what a pretty pack on 'e! Here, come along wi' me, and we'll zee what we can vind th'.'

The child required no second bidding, but followed the farmer to the dairy door, where a hunk of bread and cheese was placed in his hand. The poor little creature began to eat voraciously, for he had but a scanty breakfast that morning. The farmer and his wife looked on with great satisfaction.

'Well,' said he, 'woot like anything else?'

'Eez,' replied the boy, grinning.

'Ha! what?' – 'A drap o' drink, maester.'

'Well, th' sha't ha' 't. Here, dame, gwo an draw'n a leetle drap.'

Little Jack Pinneger had fallen into good hands: the farmer and his wife were two creatures of most benevolent disposition. Theirs was a house from which the hungry and needy never went empty away, at which no beggar ever asked in vain; and it may be safely averred, that more charity was dispensed from their hospitable door than from any rich man's in the country. Master Large and his kind-hearted wife had never been blessed with offspring, but they were seldom without some relative's child, and, being of easy and yielding dispositions, they were sponged upon on every occasion. It happened that they had a nephew's boy staying with them at this time, and some of his cast-off clothes were luckily of a size that exactly fitted little Jack Pinneger, who marched off in his new rigging, delighted with his good luck. It may be readily imagined that, after this kind reception, Jack Pinneger often found his way to the house where he had been so well treated. He was a tall child for his age, but by no means a bright one, as will hereafter be shown. In the following year, Farmer Large thought of trying him as a bird-keeper, and accordingly set him to watch some peas. Jack was greatly elated at this appointment; for two or three days previous to entering upon his office he could talk of nothing else among his playfellows in the village. At length he was led to the ground by the honest farmer, and told to 'watch' it carefully.

Jack Pinneger did watch. He watched, and saw that a multitude of almost every denomination came to devour the farmer's peas: house-sparrows and hedge-sparrows, linnets, redstarts, tomtits, and the whole of the tribe of finches, battened on the crop uninterrupted, while the

EASTERTON

'watcher' lay under the hedge out of the hot sun, and amused himself by stripping the green bark off the stick which he had cut with his pocket-knife.

Jack marched home in the evening, delighted with his job, which he thought a very easy one. In the morning he was up and off to the field again; but he found the birds were up before him, and were eating away as if they had had nothing the previous day; in fact, by the evening, they had nearly rendered a bird-keeper needless. The watcher was just about go home, when he espied his employer approaching.

As the farmer entered the ground, he saw, to his great consternation, a very cloud of birds rise from his crop, and he involuntarily uttered a malediction on the boy, who now came running towards him.

'Maester,' said Jack, 'where be I to drive they birds to next? They've yeat up all them peazen!'

The worthy farmer made no reply, but darting on the boy a look of terrible import, rushed to the hedge to procure a twig wherewith to administer a little wholesome correction to his unworthy servant. Jack took the hint and bolted.

*John Akerman*

## TALE OF A TITLARK

A canary in a cage hanging in the kitchen served to introduce the subject of birds captive and birds free. I said that I liked the little yellow bird, and was not vexed to see him in a cage, since he was cage-born; but I considered that those who caught wild birds and kept them prisoners did not properly understand things. This happened to be Caleb's view. He had a curiously tender feeling about the wild birds, and one amusing incident of his boyhood which he remembered came out during our talk. He was out on the down one summer day in charge of his father's flock, when two boys of the village on a ramble in the hills came and sat down on the turf by his side. One of them had a titlark, or meadow pipit, which he had just caught, in his hand, and there was a hot argument as to which of the two was the lawful owner of the poor little captive. The facts were as follows. One of the boys having found the nest became possessed with the desire to get the bird. His companion at once offered to catch it for him, and together they withdrew to a distance and sat down and waited until the bird returned to sit on the eggs. Then the young birdcatcher returned to the spot, and creeping quietly up to within five or six feet of the nest threw his hat so that it fell over the sitting titlark; but after having

thus secured it he refused to give it up. The dispute waxed hotter and they sat there, and at last when it got to the point of threats of cuffs on the ear and slaps on the face they agreed to fight it out, the victor to have the titlark. The bird was then put under a hat for safety on the smooth turf a few feet away, and the boys proceeded to take off their jackets and roll up their shirt-sleeves, after which they faced one another, and were just about to begin when Caleb, thrusting out his crook, turned the hat over and away flew the titlark.

The boys, deprived of their bird and of an excuse for a fight, would have discharged their fury on Caleb, but they durst not, seeing that his dog was lying at his side; they could only threaten and abuse him, call him bad names, and finally put on their coats and walk off.

*W.H. Hudson*

## OX PLOUGH

As to methods of agriculture, 'sod burning' supplemented the manuring of the land by sheep. The surface of the turf was skimmed off with a breast plough, piled loosely in heaps, lighted at the top and allowed to smoulder. Then, when ploughing was over, seed and ashes were broadcast together. Such a practice too freely followed impoverished the land, but on the downs 'sod-burning' continued for a long time. The plough most favoured in Wiltshire was the heavy western sallow, usually with two wheels but sometimes only one, and for the wetter land a one-footed affair.

Sometimes a weighted thornbush served as a harrow which, provided the soil was dry enough, worked very well. Both horses and oxen were used for ploughing and harrowing, but whereas on the steeper upland fields, such as Dicklesbury or Honey Furlong, horses would have been more popular, for the low-lying fields the ox was considered the better beast. In his attractive *The Secret People*, Mr Martin writes: 'Ploughmen in the fields worked happily in pairs, chanting softly to their oxen in local dialect, with inflexions that the beasts understood. To them the lumbering oxen with their splayed feet and rolling gait were the ideal beasts for ploughing,' and he goes on to quote 'Old Fitzherbert' – 'Therefore, meseemes, all thynges considered, the ploughe of oxen is much more profitable than the plough of horses.' Oxen were cheaper to feed and steadier, even if slower. A few Wiltshire farmers still clung to them even as late as the end of the nineteenth century. I remember, as a small child, climbing up from the canal near Horton and as I scrambled through the hedge meeting the staring, patient eyes of a pair of white oxen yoked to a plough.

*Ida Gandy*

BAT AND BALL INN, WOODFALLS

## A DRAP O' ZUMMUT

It's oondervul to me how thengs *do* move about whenever a body's got a drap o' zummut in's yead. Last harrest, a'ter zupper, at th' house yander, I walked whoam by myzelf, and zeed the moon and the zeven stars dancin' away like vengeance. Then they there girt elmen trees in the close was a dancin' away like Bill Iles and his mates at a morris. My zarvice to 'e,' zays I; 'I haups you won't tread on my twoes;' zo I went drough a sheard in th' hedge, instead o' goin' drough th' geat. Well, when I got whoam, I managed to vind the kay-hole o' th' doower – but 'twas a lang time afore I could get un to bide still enough, – and got up stayers. Massy upon us! the leetle table (I zeed un very plain by the light o' th' moon) was runnin' round th' room like mad, and there was th' two owld chayers runnin' a'ter he, and by and by, round comes the bed a'ter they two. 'Ha! ha!' zays I, 'that's very vine; but how be I to lay down while you cuts zich capers?' Well, the bed comed round dree times, and the vowerth time I drowd myzelf flump atop ov un; but in th' marnin' I vound myzelf laying on the vloor, wi' ael me duds on! I never *could* make out this.

*John Akerman*

## JOHN BROWN

'John Brown is dead,' said an aged friend and visitor in answer to my inquiry for the strong labourer.

'Is he really dead?' I asked, for it seemed impossible.

'He is. He came home from his work in the evening as usual, and seemed to catch his foot on the threshold and fell forward on the floor. When they picked him up he was dead.'

I remember the doorway; a raised piece of wood ran across it, as is commonly the case in country cottages, such as one might easily catch one's foot against if one did not notice it; but he knew that bit of wood well. The floor was of brick, hard to fall on and die. He must have come down over the crown of the hill, with his long slouching stride, as if his legs had been half pulled away from his body by his heavy boots in the furrows when a ploughboy. He must have turned up the steps in the bank to his cottage, and so, touching the threshold, ended. He is gone through the great doorway, and one pencil-mark is rubbed out. There used to be a large hearth in that room, a larger room than in most cottages; and when the fire was lit, and the light shone on the yellowish red brick beneath and the large rafters overhead, it was homely and pleasant. In summer the door was always wide open. Close by on the

16

JOB (JOHN) BROWN'S HOUSE, COATE

high bank there was a spot where the first wild violets came. You might look along miles of hedgerow, but there were never any until they had shown by John Brown's.

If a man's work that he has done all the days of his life could be collected and piled up around him in visible shape, what a vast mound there would be beside some! If each act or stroke was represented, say by a brick, John Brown would have stood the day before his ending by the side of a monument as high as a pyramid. Then if in front of him could be placed the sum and product of his labour, the profit to himself, he could have held it in his clenched hand like a nut, and no one would have seen it. Our modern people think they train their sons to strength by football and rowing and jumping, and what are called athletic exercises; all of which it is the fashion now to preach as very noble, and likely to lead to the goodness of the race. Certainly feats are accomplished and records are beaten, but there is no real strength gained, no hardihood built up. Without hardihood it is of little avail to be able to jump an inch farther than somebody else. Hardihood is the true test, hardihood is the ideal, and not these caperings or ten minutes' spurts.

Now, the way they made the boy John Brown hardy was to let him roll about on the ground with naked legs and bare head from morn till night, from June till December, from January till June. The rain fell on his head, and he played in wet grass to his knees. Dry bread and a little lard was his chief food. He went to work while he was still a child. At half-past-three in the morning he

was on his way to the farm stables, there to help feed the cart-horses, which used to be done with great care very early in the morning. The carter's whip used to sting his legs, and sometimes he felt the butt. At fifteen he was no taller than the sons of well-to-do people at eleven; he scarcely seemed to grow at all till he was eighteen or twenty, and even then very slowly, but at last became a tall big man. That slouching walk, with knees always bent, diminished his height to appearance; he really was the full size, and every inch of his frame had been slowly welded together by this ceaseless work, continual life in the open air, and coarse hard food. This is what makes a man hardy. This is what makes a man able to stand almost anything, and gives a power of endurance that can never be obtained by any amount of gymnastic training.

I used to watch him mowing with amazement. Sometimes he would begin at half-past two in the morning, and continue till night. About eleven o'clock, which used to be the mowers' noon, he took a rest on a couch of half-dried grass in the shade of the hedge. For the rest, it was mow, mow, mow for the long summer day.

John Brown was dead: died in an instant at his cottage door. I could hardly credit it, so vivid was the memory of his strength. The gap of time since I had seen him last had made no impression on me; to me he was still in my mind the John Brown of the hayfield; there was nothing between then and his death.

*Richard Jefferies*

POTTER'S BUS, MARKET LAVINGTON.

CELEBRATING THE NEW FOUNTAIN, DEVIZES

## UNVEILING OF THE ESTCOURT MEMORIAL

Tuesday last was a day which the youngest amongst us will never forget, and of which the oldest will probably never see the like.

The memorial has been practically completed for some weeks, but circumstances did not allow of its being inaugurated on an earlier day. It had already become a familiar object before the ceremony of opening it was performed, and the people of Devizes had formed a somewhat premature opinion as to its claim to be regarded as an architectural success, and also as to its pretentions to merit as a fountain. It must be confessed that the public judgment had not been very favourable; though had the opportunity of inspecting it not been presented until it was complete in all its details, the verdict probably might not have been so decided. In many respects the memorial is entitled to admiration, and had it not been for some unfortunate defects in its capacity for discharging suitable jets and cascades of water, other incongruities might not have been so palpable.

Some modification had to be adopted, and the most feasible alternative plan which suggested itself was the giving of the jets an upward direction, thus ensuring the after descent of the water within its prescribed limits. Upon two of the outflow tubes, after their alteration, were affixed rose nozzles, and a much more pretty effect was at once produced, the water issuing forth in spreading jets, descending in spray. The effects of the display, after these modifications, was much more pleasing than had been anticipated, and probably even if it its not all that might have been hoped, the fountain will be deemed a not unworthy addition to the architectural features of the old town. The statue, which is carved in hard Portland stone,

DEVIZES

represents Mr. Sotheron Estcourt in the attitude of addressing an assembly; the right hand partially elevated; while in the left is borne a rolled document. The figure, which is of life size, and stands facing the south, was executed by Nicholl of London, and is unanimously pronounced to bear a remarkably faithful likeness to the gentleman whose memory it perpetuates. The inscription which is carried round the large basin runs thus; – 'Erected 1879, by public subscription, to the memory of the Right Hon. Thomas H.S. Sotheron Estcourt, member of Parliament for Marlborough, Devizes and North Wilts for a period of 33 years, Founder of the Wilts Friendly Society.'

A public dinner, at which many ladies were present, was held in the Corn Exchange shortly after the ceremony, under the presidency of Lord Nelson. It had been understood for some days previously that the demand for tickets was very active, and the committee were much exercised as to how the requisite accommodation should be provided, but by utilizing the space in the hall to the utmost, about eight hundred persons were seated, including about fifty who dined in the gallery, where the Devizes string band was also stationed, and performed some excellent music during and after dinner, their services being rendered gratuitously.

The illuminations were looked forward to with eager anticipations, and as a service of late trains was put on most of the visitors were enabled to remain and witness the spectacle. The fountain, illuminated with the parabolic light, was to be the *piece de resistance* of the evening, and accordingly as dusk set in all whose curiosity had been sufficiently aroused by the graphic account which had been circulated of the wonderful process whereby the fountain could be decked in 'all the colours of the rainbow' – that was everybody – pressed onwards towards the Market Place, where the transformation was to be performed. The artist, Mr. Rudge of Bath, did not keep them in suspense, for as soon as the desirable degree of obscurity – apologising to the Gas Company for using the exprssion – had overshadowed the town, all the glories of the parabolic light shone forth, and the object on which all eyes were directed, assumed the appearance of a fountain of molten silver. Mr. Rudge fulfilled all his promises, and the spectators were delighted with the many varied tints and brilliant effects which were produced. The exhibition was continued throughout the whole evening, and afforded abundant gratification to those who thronged the Market Place.

*Devizes and Wiltshire Gazette, 18 September 1879*

WEST FARM, AVEBURY

## OLD WAYS

Every day something new is introduced into farming, and yet the old things are not driven out. Every one knows that steam is now used on the farm for ploughing and threshing and working machinery at the farmstead, and one would have thought that by this time it would have superseded all other motive powers. Yet this very day I counted twenty great cart-horses at work in one ploughed field. They were all in pairs, harnessed to harrows, rollers, and ploughs, and out of the twenty, nineteen were dark-coloured. Huge great horses, broad of limb, standing high up above the level surface of the open field, great towers of strength, almost prehistoric in their massiveness. Enough of them to drag a great cannon up into a battery on the heights. The day before, passing the same farm – it was Sunday – a great bay cart-horse mare standing contentedly in a corner of the yard looked round to see who it was going by, and the sun shone on the glossy hair, smooth as if it had been brushed, the long black mane hung over the arching neck, the large dark eyes looked at us so quietly – a real English picture. The black funnel of the steam-engine has not driven the beautiful cart-horses out of the fields. They have been there for centuries, and there they stay; the notched, broad wheel of the steam-plough has but just begun to leave its trail on the earth. New things come, but the old do not go away. One life is but a summer's day

compared with the long cycle of years of agriculture, and yet it seems that a whole storm, as it were, of innovations has burst upon the fields ever since I can recollect, and, as years go, I am still in the green leaf. The labouring men used to tell me how they went reaping, for although you may see what is called reaping still going on at harvest-time, it is not reaping. True reaping is done with a hook alone and the hand; all the present reaping is 'vagging,' with a hook in one hand and a bent stick in the other, and instead of drawing the hook towards him and cutting it, the reaper chops at the straw as he might at an enemy. Then came the reaping machines, that simply cut the wheat, and left it lying flat on the ground, which were constantly altered and improved. Now there are the wire and string binders, that not only cut the corn, but gather it together and bind it in sheaves – a vast saving in labour. Still the reaping-hook endures and is used on all small farms, and to some extent on large ones, to round off the work of the machine; the new things come, but the old still remains. In itself the reaping-hook is an enlarged sickle, and the sickle was in use in Roman times, and no man knows how long before that. With it the reaper cut off the ears of the wheat only, leaving the tall straw standing, much as if it had been a pruning-knife. It is the oldest of old implements – very likely it was made of a chip of flint at first, and then of bronze, and then of steel, and now at Sheffield or Birmingham in its enlarged form of the 'vagging' hook. In the hand of Ceres it was the very

SILBURY HILL

symbol of agriculture, and that was a goodly time ago. At this hour they say the sickle is still used in several parts of England where the object is more to get the straw than the ear.

*Richard Jefferies*

## WINDFALL

One Sunday morning Caleb was on his way to his ewes folded at a distance from the village, walking by a hedgerow at the foot of the down, when he heard a shot fired some way ahead, and after a minute or two a second shot. This greatly excited his curiosity and caused him to keep a sharp look-out in the direction the sounds had come from, and by and by he caught sight of a man walking towards him. It was Old Gaarge in his long smock-frock, proceeding in a leisurely way towards the village, but catching sight of the shepherd he turned aside through a gap in the hedge and went off in another direction to avoid meeting him. No doubt, thought Caleb, he has got his gun in two pieces hidden under his smock. He went on until he came to a small field of oats which had grown badly and had only been half reaped, and here he discovered that Old Gaarge had been lying in hiding to shoot at the partridges that came to feed. He had been screened from the sight of the birds by a couple of hurdles and some straw, and there were feathers of the birds he had shot scattered about. He had finished his Sunday morning's sport and was going back, a little too late on this occasion as it turned out.    Caleb went on to his flock, but before getting to it his dog discovered a dead partridge in the hedge; it had flown that far and then dropped, and there was fresh blood on its feathers. He put it in his pocket and carried it about most of the day while with his sheep on the down. Late in the afternoon he spied two magpies pecking at something out in the middle of a field and went to see what they had found. It was a second partridge which Old Gaarge had shot in the morning and had lost, the bird having flown to some distance before dropping. The magpies had probably found it already dead, as it was cold; they had begun tearing the skin at the neck and had opened it down the breast-bone. Caleb took this bird, too, and by and by, sitting down to examine it, he thought he would try to mend the torn skin with the needle and thread he always carried inside his cap. He succeeded in stitching it neatly up, and putting back the feathers in their place the rent was quite concealed. That

21

PEWSEY

evening he took the two birds to a man in the village who made.a livelihood by collecting bones, rags, and things of that kind; the man took the birds in his hand, held them up, felt their weight, examined them carefully, and pronounced them to be two good, fat birds, and agreed to pay two shillings for them.

Such a man may be found in most villages; he calls himself a 'general dealer', and keeps a trap and pony – in some cases he keeps the ale-house – and is a useful member of the small, rural community – a sort of human carrion-crow.

*W.H. Hudson*

## JACKDAW

At one end of the Wiltshire village where I was staying there was a group of half-a-dozen cottages surrounded by gardens and shade trees, and every time I passed this spot on my way to and from the downs on that side, I was hailed by a loud challenging cry – a sort of 'Hullo, who goes there!' Unmistakably the voice of a jackdaw, a pet bird no doubt, friendly and impudent as one always expects Jackie to be. And as I always like to learn the history of every pet daw I come across, I went down to the cottage the cry usually came from to make enquiries. The door was opened to me by a tall, colourless, depressed-

looking woman, who said in reply to my question that she didn't own no jackdaw. There was such a bird there, but it was her husband's and she didn't know nothing about it. I couldn't see it because it had flown away somewhere and wouldn't be back for a long time. I could ask her husband about it; he was the village sweep, and also had a carpenter's shop.

I did not venture to cross-question her; but the history of the daw came to me soon enough – on the evening of the same day, in fact. I was staying at the inn and had already become aware that the bar-parlour was the customary meeting-place of a majority of the men in that small isolated centre of humanity. There was no club nor institute or reading-room, nor squire or other predominant person to regulate things differently. The landlord, wise in his generation, provided newspapers liberally as well as beer, and had his reward. The people who gathered there of an evening included two or three farmers, a couple of professional gentlemen – not the vicar – a man of property, the postman, the carrier, the butcher, the baker and other tradesmen, the farm and other labourers, and last, but not least, the village sweep. A curious democratic assembly to be met with in a rural village in a purely agricultural district, extremely conservative in politics.

I had already made the acquaintance of some of the people, high and low, and on that evening, hearing much hilarious talk in the parlour, I went in to join the company,

FISHERTON DE LA MERE

and found fifteen or twenty persons present. The conversation, when I found a seat, had subsided into a quiet tone, but presently the door opened and a short, robust-looking man with a round, florid, smiling face looked in upon us.

'Hullo, Jimmy, what makes you so late?' said someone in the room. 'We're waiting to hear the finish of all that trouble about your bird at home. Stolen any more of your wife's jewellery? Come in, and let's hear all about it.'

'Oh, give him time,' said another. 'Can't you see his brain's busy inventing something new to tell us!'

'Inventing, you say!' exclaimed Jimmy, with affected anger. 'There's no need to do that! That there bird does tricks nobody would think of.'

Here the person sitting next to me, speaking low, informed me that this was Jimmy Jacob, the sweep, that he owned a pet jackdaw, known to everyone in the village, and supposed to be the cleverest bird that ever was. He added that Jimmy could be very amusing about his bird.

'I'd already begun to feel curious about that bird of yours,' I said, addressing the sweep. 'I'd like very much to hear his history. Did you take him from the nest?'

'Yes, Jim,' said the man next to me. 'Tell us how you came by the bird; it's sure to be a good story.'

Jimmy, having found seat and had amung of beer put before him, began by remarking that he knew someone had been interesting himself in that bird of his. 'When I went home to tea this afternoon,' he continued, 'my missus, she says to me: "There's that bird of yours again," she says.

'"What bird?" says I. "If you mean Jack," says I "what's he done now? – out with it!"

'"We'll talk about what he's done bime-by," says she. "What I mean is, a gentleman called to ask about that bird."

'"Oh, did he?" says I. "Yes," she says. "I told him I didn't know nothing about it. He could go and ask you. You'd be sure to tell him a lot."

'"And what did the gentleman say to that?" says I.

'"He arsked me who you was, an' I said you was the sweep an' you had a carpenter's shop near the pub, and was supposed to do carpentering."

'*Supposed* to do carpentering! That's how she said it.

'"And what did the gentleman say to that?' says I.

'"He said he thought he seen you at the inn, and I said that's just where he would see you.'

'"Anything more between you and the gentleman?" says I, and she said: "No, nothing more except that he said he'd look you up, and arst if you was a funny little fat man, sort of round, with a little red face. And I said, 'Yes, that's him.'"'

Here I thought it time to break in. 'It's true,' I said, 'I called at your cottage and saw your wife, but there's no truth in the account you've given of the conversation I had with her.'

AVEBURY

There was a general laugh. 'Oh, very well,' said Jimmy. 'After that I've nothing more to say about the bird or anything else.'

I replied that I was sorry, but we need not begin our acquaintance by quarrelling – that it would be better to have a drink together.

Jimmy smiled consent, and I called for another pint for Jimmy and a soda for myself; then added I was so sorry he had taken it that way as I should have liked to hear how he got his bird.

He answered that if I put it that way he wouldn't mind telling me. And everybody was pleased, and we composed ourselves once more to listen.

'How I got that there bird was like this,' he began. 'It were about half after four in the morning, summer before last, an' I was just having what I may call my beauty sleep, when all of a sudding there came a most thundering rat-a-tat-tat at the door.

'"Good Lord," says my missus, "whatever is that?"

'"Sounds like a knock at the door," says I. "Just slip on your thingamy an' go see."

'"No," she says, "you must go; it might be a man."

'"No," I says, "it ain't nothing of such consekince as that. It's only an old woman come to borrow some castor oil."

'So she went and bime-by comes back and says: "It's a man that's called to see you an' it's very important."

'"Tell him I'm in bed," says I, "and can't get up till six o'clock."

'Well, after a lot of grumbling, she went again, then came back and says the man won't go away till he seen me, as it's very important. "Something about a bird," she says.

'"A bird!" I says, "what d'you mean by a bird?"

'"A rook," she says.

'"A rook!" says I. "Is he a madman, or what?"

'"He's a man at the door," she says, "an' he won't go away till he sees you, so you'd better git up and see him."

'"All right, old woman," I says, "I'll git up as you say I must, and I'll smash him. Get me something to put on," I says.

'"No," she says, "don't smash him"; and she give me smething to put on, weskit and trousers, so I put on the weskit and got one foot in a slipper, and went out to him with the trousers in my hand. And there he was at the door, sure enough, a tramp!

'"Now, my man," says I, very severe-like, "what's this something important you've got me out of bed at four of the morning for? Is it the end of the world, or what?'

He looked at me quite calm and said it was something important but not that – not the end of the world. "I'm sorry to disturb you," he says, "but women don't understand things properly," he says, "an' I always think it best to speak to a man."

'"That's all very well," I says, "but how long do you intend to keep me here with nothing but this on?"

'"I'm just coming to it," he says, not a bit put out. "It's like this," he says, "I'm from the north – Newcastle way – an' on my way to Dorchester, looking for work," he says.

ALLINGTON

"'Yes, I see you are!" says I, looking him up and down, fierce-like.

"'Last evening," he says, "I come to a wood about a mile from this 'ere village, and I says to myself, 'I'll stay here and go on in the morning.' So I began looking about and found some fern and cut an armful and made a bed under a oak-tree. I slep' there till about three this morning. When I opened my eyes, what should I see but a bird sitting on the ground close to me! I no sooner see it than I says to myself, 'That bird is as good as a breakfast,' I says. So I just put out my hand and copped it. And here it is!" And out he pulled a bird from under his coat.

"'That's a young jackdaw," I says.

"'You may call it a jackdaw if you like," says he; "but what I want you to understand is that it ain't no or'nary bird. It's a bird," he says, "that'll do you han'som' and you'll be proud to have, and I've called here to make you a present of it. All I want is a bit of bread, a pinch of tea, and some sugar to make my breakfast in an hour's time when I git to some cottage by the road where they got a fire lighted," he says.

'When he said that, I burst out laughing, a foolish thing to do, mark you, for when you laugh you're done for; but I couldn't help it for the life of me. I'd seen many tramps but never such a cool one as this.

'I no sooner laughed than he put the bird in my hands, and I had to take it. "Good Lord!" says I. Then I called to the missus to fetch me the loaf and a knife, and when I got it I cut him off half the loaf. "Don't give him that,' she says; "I'll cut him a piece." But all I says was, "Go and git me the tea."

"'There's a very little for breakfast," she says. But I made her fetch the caddy, and he put out his hand and I half filled it with tea. "Isn't that enough?" says I; "well, then, have some more," I says; and he had some more. Then I made her fetch the bacon and began cutting him rashers. "One's enough," says the old woman. "No," says I, "let him have a good breakfast. The bird's worth it," says I, and went on cutting him bacon. "Anything more?" I arst him.

"'If you've a copper or two to spare," he says, "it'll be a help to me on my way to Dorchester."

"'Certainly," says I, and I began to feel in my trouser pockets and found a florin. "Here," I says, "it's all I have, but you're more than welcome to it."

'Then my missus she giv' a sort of snort, and walked off.

"'And now," says I, "per'aps you won't mind letting me go back to git some clothes on."

"'In one minute," he says, and went on calmly stowing the things away, and when he finished, he looks at me quite serious, and says, "I'm obliged to you," he says, "and I hope you haven't ketched cold standing with your feet on them bricks and nothing much on you," he says.

PEWSEY

"But I want most particular to arst you not to forget to remember about that bird I giv' you," he says. "You call it a jackdaw, and I've no particular objection to that, only don't go and run away with the idea that it's just an or'nary jackdaw. It's a different sort, and you'll come to know its value bime-by, and that it ain't the kind of bird you can buy with a bit of bread and a pinch of tea," he says. "And there's something else you've got to think of – that wife of yours. I've been sort of married myself and can feel for you," he says. "The time will come when that there bird's pretty little ways will amuse her, and last of all it'll make her smile, and you'll get the benefit of that," he says. "And you'll remember the bird was giv' to you by a man named Jones – that's my name, Jones – walking from Newcastle to Dorchester, looking for work. A poor man, you'll say, down on his luck, but not one of the common sort, not a greedy, selfish man, but a man that's always trying to do something to make others happy," he says.

'And after that, he said "Good-bye," without a smile, and walked off.

'And there at the door I stood, I don't know how long, looking after him going down the road. Then I laughed; I don't know that I ever laughed so much in my life, and at last I had to sit down on the bricks to go on laughing more comfortably, until the missus came and arst me, sarcastic-like, if I'd got the high-strikes, and if she'd better get a bucket of water to throw over me.

"I says, 'No, I don't want no water. Just let me have my laugh out and then it'll be all right.' 'Well, I don't see nothing to laugh at,' she says. 'And I s'pose you thought you giv' him a penny. Well, it wasn't a penny, it was a florin,' she says.

'"And little enough, too," I says. "What that man said to me, to say nothing of the bird, was worth a sovereign. But you are a woman, and can't understand that," I says. "No," she says, "I can't, and lucky for you, or we'd 'a' been in the workhouse before now," she says.

'And that's how I got the bird.'

*W.H. Hudson*

## THE END OF THE LINE

The workhouse, dingy and drab-looking, lies off the road somewhat, sixty or seventy paces. The entrance to it is barred with stout iron gates, which are generally fastened and locked, day and night as well. High elm-trees oversha-dow the entrance, and continue in a line along the hedgerow there. Just within is the porter's lodge – a little hut big enough to contain two persons – fitted with a stove for use in cold weather; to the right and left, before the house, are some shrubs and evergreens, which look almost black from the road. On the one hand, going in, is a patch of turf with goal-posts, where the juvenile paupers forget their situation in the excitement of a game occasionally; on

PEWSEY WORKHOUSE

the other, are gardens for flowers and vegetables. Farther down on the left are outhouses and buildings where the tramps and roadsters, who are admitted for the night, pay off their score the next morning with a little healthy exercise with the saw and hatchet, or other implement. Beyond that is more ground for vegetables, worked by the permanent 'staff' of the place. Here is the school play-yard, walled round, and fenced in with iron railings like a prison; this is the shoemaker's, and there is the tailor's shop. In the front part are the master's quarters, the Board-room, and the offices; adjoining these is the work-house proper, where the paupers are confined. The infirmary is a new building, and is situated at the rear.

The greater portion of the tragedy is here, for those detained in the other parts, though poor and unfortunate, are able-bodied enough; these are doubly wretched, in that they have no possessions of any sort, and are afflicted with diseases as well, more often of a permanent kind: there is no hope of escape for them.

*Alfred Williams*

## WORKHOUSE

The thatched cottage stood beside the road at one end of a long narrow garden, enclosed from the highway by a hedge of elder. At the back there was a ditch and mound with elm-trees, and green meadows beyond. A few poles used to lean against the thatch, their tops rising above the ridge, and close by was a stack of thorn faggots. In the garden three or four aged and mossgrown apple-trees stood among the little plots of potatoes, and as many plum-trees in the elder hedge. One tall pear-tree with scored bark grew near the end of the cottage; it bore a large crop of pears, which were often admired by the people who came along the road, but were really hard and woody. As a child he played in the ditch and hedge, or crept through into the meadow and searched in the spring for violets to offer to the passers-by; or he swung on the gate in the lane and held it open for the farmers in their gigs, in hope of a half-penny.

As a lad he went forth with his father to work in the fields, and came home to the cabbage boiled for the evening meal. It was not a very roomy or commodious home to return to after so many hours in the field, exposed to rain and wind, to snow, or summer sun. The stones of the floor were uneven, and did not fit at the edges. There was a beam across the low ceiling, to avoid which, as he grew older, he had to bow his head when crossing the apartment. A wooden ladder, or steps, not a staircase proper, behind the white-washed partition, led to the bed-room. The steps were worm-eaten and worn. In the sitting-room the narrow panes of the small window were so overgrown with woodbine as to admit but little light. But in summer the door was wide open, and the light and the soft air came in. The thick walls and thatch kept it

MALMESBURY CROSS

warm and cosy in winter, when they gathered round the fire. Every day in his manhood he went out to the field; every item, as it were, of life centred in that little cottage. In time he came to occupy it with his own wife, and his children in their turn crept through the hedge, or swung upon the gate. They grew up, and one by one went away, till at last he was left alone.

After all the ploughing and the sowing, the hoeing and the harvest, comes the miserable end. Strong as the labourer may be, thick-set and capable of immense endurance; by slow degrees that strength must wear away. The limbs totter, the back is bowed, and dimmed sight can no longer guide the plough in a straight furrow, nor the weak hands wield the reaping-hook. Hodge, who, Atlas- like, supported upon his shoulders the agricultural world, comes in his old age under the dominion of his last masters at the work-house. There, indeed, he finds almost the whole array of his rulers assembled. Tenant farmers sit as the guardians of the poor for their respective parishes; the clergyman and the squire by virtue of their office as magistrates; and the tradesman as guardian for the market town. Here are representatives of almost all his masters, and it may seem to him a little strange that it should require so many to govern such feeble folk.

*Richard Jefferies*

## GRAMFER SHAANT GOO INTA WIRKHOUSE

Nunno! a shaant goo inta Wirkhouse
   While I've a crowst a bread,
An can manage var ta keep
   A roof auver me yead.

As long as I have got me health,
   An straingth ta yarn a shillin,
An tha parish voke ull low a bit,
   Ta keep un I be willin.

An if tha wunt, I'd zooner pinch
   Than zee un goo up there,
Aelthough 'tis baddish times anuff,
   An nuthen I've ta speare.

Var poor woold man he's haighty two,
   His hair's as white as snow,
An totterin is his gait an step,
   A da sheak an trimble zo.

Mworn zixty years a shepperdin
   A wur apon tha plaain,
As bwoy, an man, a tenden sheep
   I wind an starm and rain.

STEEPLE ASHTON

An many be tha zites he've zeed,
   An many be tha tales,
What happen'd when a wur a bwoy,
   Amang thease hills an vales.

When I, a chile, how many times
   He've took I on his knee,
An twould I bout girt Wellinton,
   An his veamous victory.

An tears thay hood rin out his eyes,
   As thic tale he went droo,
Var his ony bwoy: my Fiather brave,
   Wur killed at Waterloo.

Eece, an well he caals ta mine tha day
   When tha steage coach did rattle
We lightenin speed ael droo thease vale
   We news of thic girt battle.

How, when a stopped a leetle while
   At tha public on tha green,
Tha village voke ael vlock'd aroun
   To hear tha news za keen.

And when twur know'd that Wellinton,
   Had konkerd Bonnypart,
What cheers went up, za long, an loud,
   Vrim every English heart.

HENRY JAY, BOWERCHALKE

29

SUTTON VENY

Var droo tha country Bonny's neam
  Had caas'd voke firt alarm,
An down right thankvull wur em now
  A cooden do no yarm.

An long tha thankvull cheers went up,
  An drink went vreely round,
We jay, becaas tha English voke
  Had beat the Vrenchmin zound.

Nevir avore, an nevir zunce,
  Av ther bin zich adoo,
Ael droo tha lan, as when tha news
  Did com bout Waterloo.

Var twur a glorious vite, da zaay,
  Woold zawljers, brave and hoary,
Who's livin now ta tell about
  Thic ar veam'd day a glory.

Bit when tha vlush a victory
  Had passed away again,
What mwournen did goo droo tha lan
  Var thousands that wur slain.

An when tha news rach'd Gramfer's cot
  That Fiather he wur kill'd,
What tears sur shed, what anguish keen
  Mother an Gramfer vill'd.

Bit nevir mind me lass, zaays he,
  A Fiather now I'll be,
Thy mate, my zon, died viten vur
  His king and countery.

Tha widder an tha vatherless
  A took into his cot,
An well a keer'd var bouath a we,
  Till I ta manhood got.

An shill I then, now he is woold,
  Not yeable var ta wirk,
Ze un goo hoff ta Wirkhouse,
  An me bounden duty shirk.

Nunno, a shaant goo inta Wirkhouse,
  Bit com an sheare me cot,
Tho' main scanty be me means,
  A shill have haf I got.

AMESBURY PARK

Var poor woold man he's helpless quite,
  An veeble as a chile,
His wants be vew, his heart's content,
  Var ael he've got a smile.

An shood er live a vew mwore years,
  I'll do my baste ta cheer
An brighten up his days a bit,
  As long as he be here.

In zummer, wen tha days be warm,
  In archet he shill perch,
Under tha girt elm tree an watch
  Tha voke goo inta Church.

An when tha evenins thay be vine,
  I'll vill his heart wie jay,
An teak un out amang tha zenes,
  A rambled, wen a bwoy.

I'll draa un out on top tha hill,
  In Squire's dree-wheel'd cheer,
Zo's he can look aroun wonce mwore
  On zenes that be za dear.

An wen tha gloomy winter comes,
  An vrost an snow be here,
He shill zit warm an cozy like,
  In his girt big yarm cheer.

An while tha log is burnin bright,
  Agean he shall goo droo,
His oft twould tale a Wellinton
  An tha vite at Waterloo.

Zoo a shaant goo inta Wirkhouse,
  While I've a crowst a bread,
An can manage var ta keep
  A roof auver me yead.

*Edward Slow*

31

BRANCH-LINE LOCOMOTIVE, SWINDON

## THE STAMPING SHOP

The Stamping Shop is square, or nearly so, each lateral corresponding to a cardinal point of the compass – north, south, east, and west, the whole comprising about an acre and a quarter. That is not an extensive building for a railway manufactory. There are some shops with an area of not less than five, six, and even seven acres – a prodigious size! They are used for purposes of construction, for carriages, waggons, locomotives, and also for repairs. The premises used for purely manufacturing purposes, such as those I am now speaking of, are generally much smaller in extent.

The workshop is modern in structure and has not stood for more than fifteen years. Before that time the work proceeded on a much smaller scale, and was carried on in a shed built almost entirely of wood and corrugated iron – a dark, wretched place, without light or ventilation, save for the broken windows and rents in the low, depressed roof. With the development of the industry and general expansion of trade this became altogether inadequate to cope with the requirements of the other sheds, and a move had to be made to larger and more commodious premises. Thereupon a site was chosen and a new shop erected about a quarter of a mile distant. The walls of this are of brick, built with 'piers' and 'panels,' thirty feet high, solid, massive, and substantial, with no pretence to show of any

kind. The roof is constructed in bays running north and south, according to the disposition of the long walls, and presents a serrated appearance, like the teeth of a huge saw. Of these bays the slopes towards sunrise are filled in with stout panes of glass; the opposite sides are of strong boards covered with slates, the whole supported by massive sectional principals and a network of stout iron girders.

The roof is studded with hundreds of wooden ventilators intended to carry off the smoke and fumes from the forges. Above them tower numerous furnace stacks and chimneys from the boilers, with the exhaust pipes of the engines and steam-hammers. Towards summer, when the days lengthen and the sun pours down interminable volumes of light and heat from a cloudless sky, or when the air without is charged with electricity and the thunder bellows and rolls over the hills and downs to the south, and the forked lightning flashes reveal every corner of the dark smithy so that the heat becomes almost unbearable, a large quantity of the glass is removed to aid ventilation; the heat, assisted by the ground current, rises and escapes through the roof. But when the rain comes and the heavy showers, driven at an angle by the wind, beat furiously through upon the half-naked workmen beneath, even this is not an unmixed blessing. Or when the sun shoots his hot arrows down through the openings upon the toilers at the steam-hammers and forges, as he always does twice during the morning – once before breakfast, and again at

GWR FACTORY WORKERS, SWINDON

about eleven o'clock – it is productive of increased discomfort; the sweat flows faster and the work flags. This does not last long, however. Southward goes the sun, and shade succeeds.

The eastern and western ends of the shed are almost half taken up with large sliding doors, that reach as high as to the roof. These rest on wheels which are superimposed upon iron rails, so that a child might push them backwards and forwards. Through several of the doors rails are laid to permit of engines and waggons entering with loads of material – iron and steel for the furnaces – and also for conveying away the manufactures. A narrow bogie line runs round the shed and is used for transferring materials from one part to another and to the various hydraulic presses and forges. Here and there are fixed small turntables to enable the bogies to negotiate the angles and move from track to track.

Southward the shed faces a yard of about ten acres in extent. This is bounded on every side by other workshops and premises, all built of the same dingy materials – brick, slate and iron – blackened with smoke, dust, and steam, surmounted with tall chimneys, innumerable ventilators, and poles for the telephone wires, which effectually block out all perspective. To view it from the interior is like looking around the inner walls of a fortress. There is no escape for the eye; nothing but bricks and mortar, iron and

steel, smoke and steam arising. It is ugly; and the sense of confinement within the prison-like walls of the factory renders it still more dismal to those who have any thought of the hills and fields beyond. Only in summer does it assume a brighter aspect. Then the sun scalds down on the network of rails and ashen ground with deadly intensity; the atmosphere quivers and trembles; the fine dust burns under your feet, and the steel tracks glitter under the blinding rays. The clouds of dazzling steam from the engines are no longer visible – the air being too hot to admit of condensation – and the black smoke from the furnaces and boilers hangs in the air, lifeless and motionless, like a pall, for hours and hours together.

*Alfred Williams*

## FACTORY SMITHS

Nearly all the smiths live in the town and within easy reach of their work. A few only of their number have had a rustic apprenticeship. The great majority of those in the shed have learnt the rudiments of their trade in factories, and have migrated from place to place. By living in the midst of large towns and cities, they have become almost indifferent to surroundings and are able to make them-

GWR SMITH'S SHOP, SWINDON

ALFRED WILLIAMS

selves happy and comfortable in the most crowded and uncongenial situations. For the beauties of external nature they care but little; they appear to be wholly wrapt up in and concerned with their own vocation. They nearly all belong to unions and organisations, and are the most independent of men, though they do not make a great parade of the fact. Their independence is born of self-confidence – the knowledge of their own usefulness and worth, and the strength of their position. If they should choose to leave one place they are certain of getting employment elsewhere, for a good smith is never out of work for long together. Other trades suffer considerably through slackness of employment, but there is a constant demand for smiths and hammermen. The fact is that fewer smiths and forgemen are made, in proportion to their numbers, than is the case with some other trades. The work is hard and laborious, and the life must be one of toil and sacrifice.

Although some smiths drink an enormous quantity of cold water at the forge there are others who seldom taste a drop of the liquid. If you ask them the reason why, they will tell you that it is not a wise plan to drink much cold water at work. They say that it causes cramp in the stomach, colds, rash, and itching of the skin, and add that it makes them sweat very much more than they would otherwise do. The more you drink, they say, the more

GWR WORKS, SWINDON

you want to drink, and it is but a habit acquired. If you care to use yourself to it you may work in the greatest heat and feel very few ill effects from it if you are abstemious in the taking of liquids. At the same time, the majority of smiths do drink water, and that copiously, and seem to thrive well upon it. Such as do this, and are fat and well, when spoken to upon the matter, always smile broadly and tell you it is the result of having a contented mind and of drinking plenty of cold water.

*Alfred Williams*

## THE HAUNTED COKEHEAP

There is romance in every walk of life, and legends of ghosts and spirits that frequent desolate ruins and dark places, but few would think to find such a thing as a haunted forge or coke heap, though they were believed to exist by the credulous among the night-men at the factory. 'Sammy,' the cokewheeler, had a mortal dread of the cokeheap at midnight, by reason of strange, weird noises he had heard there in the lone, dark hours, and the men at the fires often had to wait for fuel, or go and get it in for themselves. Accordingly, certain among them determined

to frighten the old man still further. For several nights in succession, at about twelve o'clock, someone scaled the big high heap at the back and waited for Samuel's return from the shed with his wheel-barrow. When he arrived the hidden one set up a loud, moaning noise and started to clamber down the pile. The coke gave way and fell with a crash, and Sammy, stuttering and stammering with a childlike simplicity and in a paroxysm of fear, rushed off and told how the 'ghost' had assailed him.

*Alfred Williams*

## HAMMERMEN

The men of the steam-hammer shed differ from the rest of the factory hands in having to work a twelve-hour day. Very often the heats are ready to draw out at meal-times, and it would be ruinous to leave them to waste in the furnace while the men went home to breakfast and dinner. Accordingly, the forger and his mates boil water in a can on the neck of the furnace, or over a piece of hot metal, and make their own tea to drink. Occasionally the mid-day meal is brought to the factory entrance by the forgeman's little son or daughter, or he may bring in a

BRIDGE STREET, SWINDON

large basin full of cooked meat and vegetables and warm it up himself. Perhaps the fare is a rasher of bacon. This the workman brings in raw and either roasts it over the furnace door, or on a lump of hot iron. Perhaps he uses a roughly-made frying-pan; or he may place it in the furnaceman's shovel in order to cook it. If the furnaceman sees him, however, he will certainly forbid this, for heating the shovel will spoil the temper of the steel and cause it to warp. He will say, moreover, that coal charged into the furnace with a shovel that has had 'that mess' in it will never heat the iron, and I have more than once seen the half-cooked food unceremoniously turned out into the coal-dust. A common name for the roughly-made frying-pan is a 'rasher-waggon.'

*Alfred Williams*

## A FORTUNATE ESCAPE ON THE GREAT WESTERN RAILWAY

Mr. A.P. Longstaffe writes from the Temple: – 'I was a passenger on Monday on the Great Western Railway from Gloucester in the last carriage but two of the train timed to leave there at 2.5 p.m. Immediately after leaving Swindon I noticed that the wheels of the carriage in which I was

seated made a peculiar hammering sound, which seemd to grow louder as we proceeded and the speed of the train was increased. After about twenty minutes I heard a loud crack, and saw a piece of red-hot metal, the size of a cricket ball, shoot from underneath the carriage across the down line, and the carriage began to oscillate and jolt violently. It being evident that some thing serious had happened to the wheels, I opened the window and kept pulling the communication cord, right into the carriage, but without producing any result whatever. Meanwhile the carriage continued to oscillate and jolt so violently that it was as much as I or any of the other occupants of the carriage could do to hold on to the seats or doors. Fortunately, after travelling some two or three miles in this fashion the driver of a goods train which we passed saw what was happening, and by his whistle attracted the attention of the driver of our train who then shut off steam, applied his brake, and so brought us to a standstill. It was then found that the carriage in question had got off the rails owing to the breaking of an axle, and it was plain that a terrible calamity had only just been averted, for there were at least 50 people in the last three carriages. Upon examining the communication cord I found that the portion of it between the damaged carriage and the van of the rear guard had broken in two (it seemed old and rotten), while the reason

REGENT STREET, SWINDON

REGENT STREET, SWINDON

AMESBURY

YOUNG FARMERS IN THE WILTSHIRE YEOMANRY

SALISBURY PLAIN

that we had been unable to attract the attention of our engine driver was that at the engine end of the fifth coach of the train the communication cord had been tied in so large a knot that it was absolutely impossible to draw it through the rings which carried it. Anything more scandalously negligent it would be indeed hard to conceive. This is, I fear, another illustration of the ridiculous inadequacy of the penalty of £10 imposed by 'The Regulation of Railways Act, 1868,' upon railway companies for 'the means of communciation between the passengers and the servants of the company in charge of the train' not being efficient.

*Devizes and Wiltshire Gazette, 9 October 1890*

## ARMY ON THE PLAIN

I have hardly touched upon the fact – unhappy from all except, perhaps, a practical point of view – that the eastern part of the Plain has been adopted of late years as a military training ground, but it cannot be ignored. There is less change, however, than might be thought. The landscape is so large and open that the camps scattered here and there from April to September – and even a permanent settlement, such as Bulford Camp – are soon lost and forgotten in its immensity. A fold in the downs, which looks from a distance a mere wrinkle in the surface, can hide a whole army corps from sight. On the other hand, the cavalry exercises are even picturesque to see, and the sound of squadrons trotting over the turf with the clangour and ring of innumerable accoutrements – like the sound of many waters – almost makes up for their intrusion. Amesbury and some of the villages suffer a good deal from the dust and disturbance of passing troops and military traffic, but the autumn rains restore sweetness and peace; and when the season of firing practice, which prohibits free wandering on the downs in the military area at certain hours of the day, is over, the shepherds feed their sheep there as usual and all is as it was, except for a few ugly tin buildings, and a hard road in places where formerly only a down track ran.

The western and southern part of the Plain remains free from invasion.

*Ella Noyes*

PERHAM DOWN CAMP, NORTH TIDWORTH

## A BATTLE SPOILED BY THE RAIN

Though this year's training of troops on Salisbury Plain began over two months ago, the dryness of the summer has been such that until Monday last there was no occasion on which the work was interfered with by rain; but on Monday a perfect deluge descended on Salisbury and the surrounding district, and it drenched the troops on the Plain and brought the operations to a premature close. It had been arranged that Monday, Tuesday and Wednesday should be interdivisional manœuvre days; and on Monday the increased importance of the operations attracted a much larger number of spectators than on any previous day. The Adjutant-General, Sir Evelyn Wood, was present, as were several other distinguished military men. Unfortunately, while the day's operations were in progress, a very heavy storm came on. The correspondent of the *Daily Graphic* remarks: – 'The downpour of rain was quite torrential, and as it was impossible to go on, the troops had to be marched back to their camps at Balford and Perham Down respectively. When the cease-firing sounded there could not have been a dry shred of clothing on anybody's back on the ground. What, indeed, must have been the condition of the unfortunate militiamen, who had no change of uniform when they got back to their tents, one dare not imagine.'

*Salisbury and Winchester Journal, 2 September 1899*

## FIRE IN DEVIZES

On Monday evening a fire broke out on the premises of Messrs. Wadworth and Co., adjoining the Royal Oak Inn, New Park Street, in a shed which has been rented by Mr. Marvin. No one appears to have any knowledge as to how the fire originated. The yard in which the burned-out shed was situated is parallel with that of the Royal Oak, and runs from New Park Street into Commercial Road, and has an entrance from both thoroughfares. On the right hand side is a long brick building with tiled roof, used by Messrs. Wadworth and Co. as a malthouse, and in it was stored a considerable quantity of malt. On the left there is also a range of buildings chiefly constructed of wood, with boarded roof. One portion of this has been used as a blacksmith's shop, and the remainder has been rented by Mr. Hayward, and used as a carpenter's shop. It is stacked with a large quantity of timber. At the end of the yard and filling up all the back portion between Mr. Hayward's shop and Messrs. Wadworth's malthouse was situated the shed in which the fire originated. It was rented by Mr. Marvin from Messrs. Wadworth & Co., and was used by him as a sort of general storehouse. In it were a horse rake, reaping machine, new waggon, and various other implements, together with a considerable quantity of hay, several tons of chaff and numerous miscellaneous articles, altogether of the value of about £150. When the fire was first noticed, shortly before six o'clock, it had got a firm

DEVIZES

hold of the shed, which was constructed chiefly of wood and had a tarred felt roofing. As soon as it was discovered a messenger was despatched for the fire brigade, which, under Mr. Randell, jun., and Mr. Lucas was quickly on the spot. By the time they arrived, however, the roof of the shed had fallen in, and the contents were a mass of flames. Two lengths of hose, one supplied from the main in New Park Street and the other from a fire-plug in Commerical Road, were speedily brought into use, and a large volume of water was poured on the burning mass. Ample volunteer help was forthcoming from persons who were attracted by the blaze, and the efforts made by persons present soon told with affect. The connection between Mr. Hayward's shop and the burning shed, which it was for a moment feared would prove a source of great disaster, was speedily severed, and thus the fire was practically confined to the limited area in which it broke out. The malthouse being built of brick with tiled roof did not sustain any serious damage, though the water did much injury to the malt stored in the basement. The firemen speedily got the flames in subjection, though it was after eight o'clock before it was quite extinguished. The shed and its contents are of course completely consumed, and the walls have almost entirely fallen in.

Fortunately, both Mr. Marvin's goods and the premises themselves are, as we are informed, fairly covered by insurance, so that the loss to Messrs. Wadworth and Mr. Marvin will not prove very serious. At the last meeting of the Urban Authority it was resolved to purchase two lengths of new hose. The resolution is none too soon, for the hose in use on Monday evening proved altogether untrustworthy, and the water was spurting from a dozen places in both the pieces used. The hose is, in fact, completely worn out.

*Devizes and Wiltshire Gazette, 10 July 1890*

## SUN BONNETS

The dwellings provided for the deserving poor were even more comely than the labourers' cottages. Ever since mediæval times there had been 'poore almswomen' maintained by the Church; and in the seventeenth century, thanks to the munificence of one Thomas Westmead, broadweaver, almshouses were built for such needy and aged persons. They are six cottages joined lengthwise, each with its gable and mullioned windows. Their front

URCHFONT

windows look out over the churchyard across the road; from their cloisters at the back, that run the whole length of the building, the almswomen can see the Manor and Priory Farm. Every afternoon when the milking is done they take their jugs and go across the field to the dairy to fetch their milk for tea. When the grass is laid up for hay and they go in single file along the narrow footpath, wearing their sun-bonnets, they look like a line of white ducks. Polly Fry, herself an almswoman, made all six bonnets, and could make them again, for all her seventy-eight years, if they should at last wear out with constant starching and goffering. She never measures any one: there is one bonnet, and she can make no other. She makes it as she was taught by her aunt, who was a lace-maker at Malmesbury, with 'poll-piece' at the back, double hood to turn back in the front, gathered 'curtain' round the neck, little bow in the nape (this has no function, but it is imperative that it should be there) and strings which always remain untied. The main part, which is gathered into the poll-piece, must have its right quota of tucks and pipings of bonnet-cotton – three rows of piping, a tuck; one row of piping, a tuck; two rows of piping, a tuck; and so on. In her younger days Polly used to be kept busy supplying the Bramelham shops: now there is no demand save from her neighbours.

*Heather and Robin Tanner*

BRATTON

BRADFORD-ON-AVON

## SHEPHERDS

Inseparable from one's thought of Salisbury Plain is its familiar spirit, the shepherd with his sheep. The pale flock moving over the low green swells, now tailing out, now rounding into bunches, the slow figure stalking beside them, anon pausing in his measured walk and leaning motionless upon his stick, while they feed round him; the dog sitting up a little apart, emulating in little that human gravity and wisdom. All the sameness and silence of the Plain is in that constant spectacle. Though the shepherd has no distinctive dress, no baldrick, sling, or flute, carries nothing more romantic than his big green umbrella and dinner basket slung upon his back – has no crook even, yet his calling gives a certain interesting character and peculiarity to his appearance. His lonely figure in the corduroys and white jacket of summer seems a very part of the pale fields and breezy sky and the sunburnt downs. But in cold or stormy winter he is more impressive. The greatcoat which he wraps about him on wild wet days hangs upon his patient form in statuesque folds. How large the dark cloaked figure looms through the driving mist of rain, upon the downs, the only human thing visible in that immensity under the grey sky. The slowness and halt of his gait has a dignity denied to the fretful units of a crowd. He should be different from other men. Are all these hours sterile that he spends alone up here? Does the shepherd think? He is not seen to read a book in the narrow sense of the word, in those seemingly idle hours. But he has a greater book always open before him, and perhaps could

SHEPHERD JACOB SOUND, LITTLE CHEVERELL

SHEEP SHEARING, BERWICK BASSETT

tell much, if he were more articulate. He has time to divine deeper than we distracted mortals may. He speaks little. A sign, and the dog springs up and racing this way and that, with barks and pretence of fury, rounds up the timid flock; the shepherd moves slowly off, who knows by what impelled? The sheep follow, cropping as they go. It is astonishing how fast they move as they feed; the fleecy backs are all round one, and the multitudinous sound of teeth tearing the grass; a minute or two later one finds oneself alone, the flock has vanished utterly behind a swell or in a fold of the down.

*Ella Noyes*

## RABBIT-WARRENS

Rabbit-warrens were formerly looked upon as a legitimate investment, and certain to produce a good income. In more than one case large fortunes are said to have been realized in this manner. The secret lay in the fact that the barren wastes devoted to this purpose could be rented at a very low rate, and that the capital required was small in amount, and yet gave a high percentage of returns. Warrens were in full prosperity just previous to the out-break of the great French wars with Napoleon I. About that time and afterwards corn rose so much in value that every available scrap of land, good or bad, meadow or heath, was ploughed up, and even if the wheat crop produced was but scanty, still it paid well. Consequently warrens fell into disuse, and though wheat is now a dangerous crop to depend upon, have never been revived on a large scale.

In Wiltshire there were many warrens on the downs, as at Aldbourne, and near Wanborough, the rabbits from which were sent to London in the huge road-waggons, drawn by several horses, which then made the journey – just such wagons as once gave Dick Whittington a lift by the way. The Aldbourne warren is still remembered, and the rabbits are said to have consumed several loads of hay a day in frosty and snowy weather.

*Richard Jefferies*

FLOODS AT ALDBOURNE

WOODBOROUGH

FISHERTON DE LA MERE

IMBER

IMBER

## IMBER

To get to Imber we must leave the road we have been pursuing at Gore Cross, and take the one which climbs south-westward over the downs, and is for a part of its way only a track in the turf. Imber – or Immere – meaning 'on the border,' from the fact that it lies on the boundary of two Hundreds – is the most isolated of all the villages on the Plain, and the loveliest and most unspoilt.

A hundred years ago and later there were no roads at all to Imber. The village lies in a deep fold of the Plain, on the track of another little winter stream; on all sides the slopes of the high downs surround it. It is just one straggling 'street' of old cottages and farmsteads, winding along the hollow under the sheltering elms; the narrow stream brims fresh and clear through it in spring, leaving its bed dry, to fill up with coarse grass and weeds, in summer. The white-washed cottages, with their leaning timbers and deep thatched roofs, are set down in short rows and groups, the angles and nooks between them filled in with garden plots full of flowers; rose bushes, here and there a lilac, lilies, and tangles of everlasting peas. There is an old timbered house about midway along the street which cannot be younger than the fourteenth century. Such barns too, there are, deep, lofty, capacious, built of grand old timbers, with a thick cape of thatch thrown over the long roof and two pockets in the thatch bulging out over the big double storied doors. The long walls of the orchards and gardens are all the old mud built kind here, rustic and comfortable under their coping of thatch.

*Ella Noyes*

*[The inhabitants of Imber were evacuated at short notice in 1943 by The Ministry of Defence which wanted the village for army training. The promise that the village would be returned after the war was never honoured and to this day it remains a military training area. Only the church survives intact.]*

## THRESHING

Very soon after harvest threshing began. The engine and machine, covered with tarpaulins, were drawn from farm to farm by strong teams of horses, three or four on each; the troops of children, boys and girls too, followed them all up the lane, greatly excited; it was wonderful to them to see the black smoke towering out of the tall iron chimney, the piston-rod shooting silently in and out, the wheels spinning round, and the long belt communicating power to the thresher, the chaff and chaving flying, and the straw rustling down behind. The humming of the thresher has a peculiar fascination as well, especially at that time of the

STEAM THRESHING, MARKET LAVINGTON

year; it sounds so mournful and plaintive borne to you over the field; it is like a dirge to the dying year, yet it is not a depressing sound at all, but exactly fits in with the surroundings of the farm and country-side.

The engine was drawn in first, then the thresher. The latter is set in position near the corn rick, and the wheels secured with wedges to prevent it from shifting under the power of the belt. Then the engine is set, too, at a certain distance, and the wheels firmly wedged as well. Sometimes shallow holes are dug for the wheels to drop in, to prevent motion, for the engine oscillates considerably under the force of the steam. The farmer supplies coal for the boiler, and must also see to the water. This is contained in a large tub close to the fire-box. Two rubber tubes are inserted from the engine; the exhaust steam is ejected from one of these, the water is injected by means of the other. There are two men in charge of the tackle one of these attends to the engine, the other feeds the thresher. Dudley Sansum and old Thomas Bowles used to do this in turns, and so equalize the labour; they were both exceedingly proud of their engine. Four sacks are suspended at the rear of the machine for catching the grain. One of these is for the most inferior, all kinds of seeds and stuff; one is for the seconds, and the other two for the firsts. This patters down from the fans within like hail-stones; it is delightful to catch it in the hand as it falls into the mouth of the sack. The Emperor Caius is said to have rolled naked in gold; I

should much prefer to roll naked in wheat. At ten, or half-past, the whistle sounds, all stop for lunch; dinner at twelve, 'little dinner' at four, bread, cheese, and ale, which is especially plentiful at threshing-time, for there is much work to be done, carrying away the straw, and one thing and the other. 'As hard as a day's dreshin';' you often hear the villagers say.

*Alfred Williams*

## A HAY HOME

At seven that evening the whole gang were collected in the farmer's great kitchen. A huge room it was, paved with stone flags, the walls whitewashed, and the ceiling being the roof itself, whose black beams were festooned with cobwebs. Three or four tables had been arranged in a row, and there was a strong smell of 'dinner' from smoking joints. Absalom came in last. He had spent some time in adorning himself in a white clean slop and new corduroys, with a gay necktie and his grand-father's watch. His face shone from a recent wash. It was an open countenance, which unconsciously prepossessed one in his favour. Light-blue or grey eyes, which looked you straight in the face, were over-shadowed with rather thick eyebrows. His forehead was well proportioned, and crowned with a mass of curling yellow hair. A profusion of whiskers hid his

RICK BUILDING

chin, which perhaps in its shape indicated a character too easy and yielding. His shoulders were broad; his appearance one of great strength. But his mouth had a sensual look. Absalom pushed in and out by Madge.

'What didst thee have to eat?' asked a crony of his afterwards.

'Aw,' said Absalom, fetching a sigh at the remembrance of the good things. 'Fust I had a plate of rus beef, then a plate of boiled beef; then I had one of boiled mutton, and next one of roast mutton; last, bacon. I found I couldn't git on at all wi' th' pudding, but when the cheese and th' salad came, didn't I pitch into that!'

Absalom's love did not spoil his appetite.

Soon as the dishes were removed pipes were brought out and tankards sent on their rounds. By this time poor old Tim's weak brains were muddled, and he was discovered leaning back against the wall and mumbling out the tag-end of an old song:–

> 'On' Humphry wi' his flail,
> But Kitty she wur the charming ma-aid
> To carry th' milking pa-ail!'

This set them on singing, and Roaring Billy insisted on bawling out at the top of his stentorian lungs the doleful ditty of 'Lord Bateman and his Daughters,' which ran to thirty verses, and lasted half-an-hour. Hardly were the last

MILL STREET, TROWBRIDGE

WARMINSTER

words out of his mouth, when an impatient wight struck up the 'Leathern Bottel,' and heartily did they all join in the chorus, down to where the ballad describes the married man wanting to beat his wife, and using a glass bottle for the purpose, which broke and let all the wine about:–

'Whereas it had been the Leathern Bottel,
The stopper been in he might banged away well,'

without danger of creating an unanswerable argument in favour of leathern bottles.

By this time they were pretty well 'boozed.' A thick cloud of tobacco-smoke filled the kitchen. Heads were rolling about from side to side and arms stretched over the tables among the *débris* of broken pipes and in pools of spilt beer and froth. Despite these rude, unromantic surroundings, Absalom and Madge were leaning close against each other, hand-in-hand, almost silent, but looking in each other's eyes.

*Richard Jefferies*

## CHORISTERS

When we were younger than the choristers we admired them very much – at least I did. To meet them in their Eton suits, ham-frills, and mortar-boards, marching briskly in procession to a Cathedral service always ranked as a spectacle. If they had had a band, it would have been better still, of course. 'Right, left, right, left', said the Bishop's boy. With the purposefulness of a train, the small, dark crocodile swung out of the sunshine into the shadow of the porch which gulped the whole lot up.

When I was as old as they were, I still admired them a little and envied them, although I pretended not to – except on one occasion when I infinitely preferred to be myself. This was when two or three of them were invited to lunch with our grandmother one Sunday. As Helen and I were their contemporaries we were supposed to hob-nob with them. But none of us could think of anything much to say to each other. They got on much better with the grown-ups, and especially with Uncle Cecil who had invited them and could talk about their sports. After lunch

and the exodus to the drawing-room, crammed with roast beef and Yorkshire pudding, three or four potatoes, cauliflower, and apple tart and custard, it was taken for granted that they should sing, to our grandmother in particular, and the rest of us thrown in. Helen and I, arranging ourselves in suitable positions to stare at them like sightseers at a Christian martyrdom, were divided between pity and a rather horrible gloating – emotions that were rendered disappointingly redundant later, when Baba told us that such a performance was as natural to them as eating and drinking.

*Geraldine Symons*

## By Carriage to the Race Plain

When our grandmother wished to see the country, a carriage was hired. But the only occasion on which I can remember this happening was the time when, to our stupendous excitement, Helen and I were invited to join the outing. There was one brown horse. Not four black. Like the waggon load on Uncle Herbert's mutton day, we went to the Race Plain. A casual ten-minute drive in a car today, that expedition, then assumed something of the

setting forth for emigration. Granny and Baba both wore dust-veils on their hats. Granny wore her tussore coat. Baba, her dust-coat. There has never been anything since quite like the sensation induced by the hot, shining, dark blue leather of that broad, shallow seat, puffed up and poked down like a pin-cushion.

Slowly, we progressed through the Close with all the importance – if not of royalty – of something that no one could fail to see as we took up most of the road. Past the scarlet letter-box, past the Choristers' Green, past the North Canonry with the great archway and garden beyond, past the Deanery, past the Choristers' Field and the Broad Walk, through the Close gate into the outside world.

Quite soon we were driving through Harnham, and up there on the left we could see Harnham Hill – the familiar long green ridge where we often went for walks. In the summer, boys hurtled down the burnt grass on tin trays. In the winter, when there was snow, people rushed down on toboggans. Children made daisy chains. Grown-ups made love. When Baba taught her Sunday school class to pray, 'Deliver us from harm and ill', they had conscientiously gabbled, 'Deliver us from 'arnham ill.'

The first flush of excitement dwindled a little after a time as the horse got slower and slower. I felt like getting out and showing it how much faster I could run. But being

THE WILLCOX FAMILY, WARMINSTER

*in* the carriage was the treat and the treat I had come out to have.

Everything was white with dust. It covered the banks and hedges like flour, spoiling the colour of the flowers. We were used to that in the country. There was no water-cart like there was in the Close. But it seemed the thickest, whitest dust I had ever seen. Baba said it was chalk and a good night's rain was needed.

When we came to the hill to the Race Plain, Granny told Helen and me to be sorry for the horse and get out and walk. We tried to feel sorry as we trudged along, but we couldn't help feeling the horse was letting us down, that a hill was the one place where we ought to ride. But at last we reached the racecourse. 'There's the grand stand!' said Baba. This, she explained, was where people sat to watch the races. There it was, indeed! – rearing up in rows of empty seats. The white railings stretched far away past the patches of golden gorse, under a blue sky with huge pillowy clouds. 'There's the spire!' Like explorers, we gazed with wonder at this distant, homely landmark.

*Geraldine Symons*

CLOSE GATE, SALISBURY

THE VICARAGE, KINGTON ST MICHAEL

## DIARY

*Thursday, 12 August*

I walked across to Kington St Michael to be present at the school feast. As we were swinging the children under the elms that crown the Tor Hill a girl came up to me with a beseeching look in her eyes and an irresistible request for a swing. She was a perfect little beauty with a plump rosy face, dark hair, and lovely soft dark eyes melting with tenderness and a sweet little mouth as pretty as a rosebud. I lifted her into the swing and away she went. But about the sixth flight the girl suddenly slipped off the swing seat feet foremost and still keeping hold of the ropes she hung from the swing helpless. Unfortunately her clothes had got hitched upon the seat of the swing and were all pulled up round her waist and it instantly became apparent that she wore no drawers. A titter and then a shout of laughter ran through the crowd as the girl's plump person was seen naked hanging from the swing. O ye gods, the fall of Hebe was nothing to it. We hustled her out of the swing and her clothes into their proper place as soon as possible and perhaps she did not know what a spectacle she had presented. I believe it was partly my fault. When I lifted the girl into the swing there were many aspirants for the seat and in the struggle and confusion I suppose I set her down with her clothes rumpled up and her bare flesh (poor child) upon the board and as her flesh was plump and smooth and in excellent whipping condition and the board slippery, they managed to part company with this result. Poor child, when she begged so earnestly for a swing she scarcely contemplated the exhibition of herself for the amusement of the spectators. I shall never see the elms on the Tor Hill now without thinking of the fall of Hebe.

*Wednesday, 25 August*

I went to Britford Vicarage to stay with the Morrises till Saturday. Late in the evening we loitered down into the water meads. The sun was setting in stormy splendour behind Salisbury and the marvellous aerial spire rose against the yellow glare like Ithuriel's spear, while the last gleams of the sunset flamed down the long lines of the water carriages making them shine and glow like canals of molten gold.

*Friday, 27 August*

To-day I paid my first visit to Stonehenge. We had breakfast before Church and immediately after service Morris and I started to walk to Stonehenge, eleven miles. Passing through the beautiful Cathedral Close and the city of Salisbury we took the Devizes road and after we had walked along that road for some six miles we saw in the dim distance the mysterious Stones standing upon the

AMESBURY CHURCH

Plain. The sun was hot, but a sweet soft air moved over the Plain 'wafting' the scent of the purple heather tufts and the beds of thyme and making the delicate blue harebells tremble on their fragile stems. A beautiful little wheatear flitted before us from one stone heap to another along the side of the wheel track as we struck across the firm elastic turf. Around us the Plain heaved mournfully with great and solemn barrows, the 'grassy barrows of the happier dead'.

Soon after we left the Druid's Head and struck across the turf eastward we came in sight of the grey cluster of gigantic Stones. They stood in the midst of a green plain, and the first impression they left on my mind was that of a group of people standing about and talking together. It seemed to me as if they were ancient giants who suddenly became silent and stiffened into stone directly anyone approached, but who might at any moment become alive again, and at certain seasons, as at midnight and on Old Christmas and Midsummers Eve, might form a true 'Chorea Gigantum' and circle on the Plain in a solemn and stately dance. It is a solemn awful place. As I entered the charmed circle of the sombre Stones I instinctively un-covered my head. It was like entering a great Cathedral Church.

Crossing the river at Normanton Hatches we walked along the hillside through meadows and barley fields till we came to the hospitable Manor House of Great Durnford, the seat of Mr John Pinckney, where we found Mr and Mrs Pinckney, Mr Charles Everett and Major Fisher, the Champion archer of England, at luncheon. After luncheon the archers went out to shoot at a beautiful archery ground by the riverside. The ladies sat watching under the trees while the arrows flashed past with a whistling rush, and the glorious afternoon sunlight shone mellow upon the beeches, and the still soft air of the river valley was filled with the cooing of woodpigeons and the strange mournful crying of the moorhens and dabchicks, and three beautiful cows came down the glade from sunlight to shadow to their milking place, and the river flashed darkly past the boathouse and under the leaning trees, and a man rowed up the stream with his milkcans in a boat from the meadows where he had milked a distant herd of cows.

*Francis Kilvert*

DEVIZES CYCLING CLUB, STONEHENGE

## DEVIZES CYCLING CLUB

A smoking concert was held on Thursday evening at the Club-room, the Bell Hotel, and proved to be the most successful that has yet been held under the auspices of the Club. The chair was taken by the President, Mr. B. Howard Cunnington, and there was a large attendance of members, for whose comfort and convenience admirable arrangements were made. The unqualified success of the concert was due, to a large extent, to the tact and judgment of Mr. Frank Cripps, upon whom devolved the responsibility of providing a programme. The proceedings went with a capital swing throughout, and were of a thoroughly enjoyable nature. A hearty vote of thanks was passed to the President for taking the chair. – At a meeting of the members, held previous to the concert, it was decided to hold a cyclist ball on the 4th March, at which the members will attend in uniform. Further particulars will be duly announced.

*Devizes and Wiltshire Gazette, 4 February 1889*

## THE KEEPER

The cottage is thatched and oddly gabled – built before 'improvements' came into fashion – yet cosy; with walls three feet thick, which keep out the cold of winter and the heat of summer. This is not solid masonry; there are two shells, as it were, filled up between with rubble and mortar rammed down hard.

Inside the door the floor of brick is a step below the level of the ground. Sometimes a peculiar but not altogether unpleasant odour fills the low-pitched sitting room – it is emitted by the roots burning upon the fire, hissing as the sap exudes and boils in the fierce heat. When the annual fall of timber takes place the butts of the trees are often left in the earth, to be afterwards grubbed and split for firewood, which goes to the great house or is sold. There still remain the roots, which are cut into useful lengths and divided among the upper employés. From elm and oak and ash, and the crude turpentine of the fir, this aromatic odour, the scent of the earth in which they grew, is exhaled as they burn.

The ceiling is low and crossed by one huge square beam of oak, darkened by smoke and age. The keeper's double-barrelled gun is suspended from this beam: there are several other guns in the house, but this, the favourite, alone hangs where it did before he had chlidren – so strong is habit; the rest are yet more out of danger. It has been a noble weapon, though now showing signs of age – the interior of the breech worn larger than the rest of the barrel from constant use; so much so that, before it was converted to a breech-loader, the wad when the ramrod pushed it down would slip the last six inches, so loosely fitting as to barely answer its purpose of retaining the shot; so that

MARLBOROUGH

when cleaned out, before the smoke fouled it again, he had to load with paper. This in a measure anticipated the 'choke-bore,' and his gun was always famous for its killing power. The varnish is worn from the stock by incessant friction against his coat, showing the real grain of the walnut-wood, and the trigger-guard with the polish of the sleeve shines like silver. It has been his companion for so many years that it is not strange he should feel an affection for it; no other ever fitted the shoulder so well, or came with such delicate precision to the 'present' position. So accustomed is he to its balance and 'hang' in the hand that he never thinks of aiming; he simply looks at the object, still or moving, throws the gun up from the hollow of his arm, and instantly pulls the trigger, staying not a second to glance along the barrel. It has become almost a portion of his body, answering like a limb to the volition of will without the intervention of reflection. The hammers are chased and elegantly shaped – perfectly matching: when once the screw came loose, and the jar of a shot jerked one off among the dead leaves apparently beyond hope of recovery, he never rested night or day till by continuous search and sifting the artistic piece of metal was found. Nothing destroys the symmetry of a gun so much as hammers which are not pairs; and well he knew that he should never get a smith to replace that delicate piece of workmanship, for this gun came originally from the hands of a famous maker, who got fifty or perhaps even seventy guineas for it years ago. It did not shoot to please the purchaser – guns of the very best character sometimes take use to get into thorough order – and was thrown aside, and so the gun became the keeper's.

These fine old guns often have a romance clinging to them, and sometimes the history is a sad one. Upstairs he still keeps the old copper powder-flask curiously chased and engraved, yet strong enough to bear the weight of the bearer, if by chance he sat down upon it while in his pocket, together with the shot-belt and punch for cutting out the wads from card-board or an old felt hat. These the modern system of loading at the breech has cast aside. Here, also, is the apparatus for filling empty cartridge-cases – a work which in the season occupies him many hours.

Being an artist in his way, he takes a pride in the shine and polish of his master's guns, which are not always here, but come down at intervals to be cleaned and attended to. And woe be to the first kid gloves that touch them afterwards; for a gun, like a sardine, should be kept in fine oil, not thickly encrusting it, but, as it were, rubbed into and oozing from the pores of the metal and wood. Paraffin is an abomination in his eyes (for preserving from rust), and no modern patent oil, he thinks, can compare with a drop of gin for the locks – the spirit never congeals in cold weather, and the hammer comes up with a clear, sharp snick. He has two or three small screwdrivers and guns-mith's implements to take the locks to pieces; for gentlemen are sometimes careless and throw their guns down on the wet grass, and if a single drop of water should by chance penetrate under the plate it will play mischief with the works, if the first speck of rust be not forthwith removed.

His dog-whistle hangs at his buttonhole. His pocket-knife is a basket of tools in itself, most probably a present

FISHERTON DE LA MERE

from some youthful sportsman who was placed under his care to learn how to handle a gun. The corkscrew it contains has seen much service at luncheon-time, when under a sturdy oak, or in a sheltered nook of the lane, where the hawthorn hedge and the fern broke the force of the wind, a merry shooting party sat down to a well-packed hamper and wanted some one to draw the corks.

*Richard Jefferies*

## BOWERCHALKE PARISH PAPERS

A Meeting of the Committee was held in the Schoolroom on Monday evening last, at which the greater part of the farmers and tradespeople of the parish shewed their interest by their absence. If a Flower Show is really a benefit to the place and people, ought it not to receive the personal interest and sympathy of those who are the employers of labour or who are otherwise in a position of responsibility? But it seems here to be the rule for the 'big people' to take no interest in anything that involves trouble or expense, until the 'little people' have overcome them both. This strikes one as being rather odd.

## ENGLISH FURS

The keeper's wife is a buxom vivacious dame, whose manners from occasional contact with the upper ranks – the ladies from the great house sometimes look in for a few minutes to chat with so old a servant of the family – are above what are usually found in her station. She receives her callers – and they are many – with a quiet, respectful dignity: desirous of pleasing, yet quite at her ease.

Across the back of the sofa there lies a rug of some beautiful fur which catches the eye, but which at first the visitor cannot identify. Its stripes are familiar, and not unlike the tiger's, but the colour is not that of the forest tyrant. She explains that this rug comes within her special sphere. It is a carriage-rug of cat-skin; the skins carefully selected to match exactly, and cured and prepared in the same way as other more famous furs. They have only just been sewn together, and the rug is now spread on the sofa to dry. She has made rugs, she will tell you, entirely of black cat-skins, and very handsome they looked; but not equal to this, which is wholly of the tabby. Certainly the gloss and stripe, the soft warmth and feel to the hand, seem to rival many foreign and costly importations. Besides carriage-rugs, the game-keeper's wife has made

LACOCK ABBEY

others for the feet – some many-coloured, like Joseph's coat.

All the cats to which these skins belonged were shot or caught in the traps set for vermin by her husband and his assistants. The majority were wild – that is, had taken up their residence in the woods, reverting to their natural state, and causing great havoc among the game. Feasting like this and in the joys of freedom, many had grown to a truly enormous size, not in fat, as the domestic animal does, but in length of back and limb. These afforded the best skins; perhaps out of eight or nine killed but two would be available or worth preserving.

She has her own receipts for preserving furs and feathers, and long practice has rendered her an adept. Here are squirrels' skins also prepared; some with the bushy tail attached, and some without. They vary in size and the colour of the tail, which is often nearly white, in others more deeply tinged with red. The fur is used to line cloaks, and the tail is sometimes placed in ladies' hats. Now and then she gets a badger-skin, which old country folk used to have made into waistcoats, said to form an efficacious protection for weak chests. She has made rugs of several sewn together, but not often.

Once or twice she has made a moleskin waistcoat for a gentleman. This is a very tedious operation. Each little skin has to be separately prepared, and when finished hardly covers two square inches of surface. Consequently it requires several scores of skins, and the work is a year or more about. There is then the sewing together, which is not to be accomplished without much patience and skill. The fur is beautifully soft and glossy, with more resemblance to velvet than is possessed by any other natural substance, and very warm. Mittens for the wrists are also made of it, and skull-caps. Moleskin waistcoats used to be thought a good deal of, but are now only met with occasionally as a curiosity.

The old wooden mole-trap is now almost extinct, superseded by the modern iron one, which anybody can set up. The ancient contrivance, a cylinder of wood, could only be placed in position by a practised hand, and from his experience in this the mole-catcher – locally called 'oont catcher' – used to be an important personage in his way. He is now fast becoming extinct also – that is, as a distinct handicraftsman spending his whole time in such trapping. He was not unfrequently a man who had once occupied a subordinate place under a keeper, and, when grown too feeble for harder labour, supported himself in this manner: contracting with the farmers to clear their fields by the season.

*Richard Jefferies*

THE WAGGON AND HORSES, BECKHAMPTON

## A COUNTRY THIRST

The great breweries whose names are household words in cities, and whose interest it is to maintain a high standard of quality for the delectation of their million consumers, do not exalt their garish painted advertisements in gilded letters as tall as Tom Thumb over the doors of village alehouses. You might call for Bass at Cairo, Bombay, Sydney, or San Francisco, and Bass would be forthcoming. But if you knocked the trestle-table with the bottom of a tankard (the correct way) in a rural public, as a signal to the cellar you might call for Bass in vain.

When the agricultural labourer drops in on his way home from his work of a winter evening – heralding his approach by casting down a couple of logs or bundle of wood which he has been carrying with a thud outside the door – he does not demand liquor of that character. When in harvest time, after sundown, when the shadows forbid further cutting with the fagging hook at the tall wheat – he sits on the form without, under the elm tree, and feels a whole pocketful of silver, flush of money like a gold digger at a fortunate rush, he does not indulge in Allsopp or Guinness. He hoarsely orders a 'pot' of some local brewer's manufacture – a man who knows exactly what he likes, and arranges to meet the hardy digestion of the mower and the reaper. He prefers a rather dark beer with a

certain twang faintly suggestive of liquorice and tobacco, with a sense of 'body,' a thickness in it, and which is no sooner swallowed than a clammy palate demands a second gulp to wash away the relics of the first. Ugh! The second requires a third swig, and still a fourth, and appetite increasing with that it feeds on, the stream rushes down the brazen throat that burns for more.

Like the Northern demi-god who drank unwittingly at the ocean from a horn and could not empty it, but nevertheless caused the ebb of the sea, so our toper, if he cannot contain the cask, will bring it down to the third hoop if time and credit will but serve. It would require a gauger's staff to measure his capacity – in fact, the limit of the labourer's liquor-power, especially in summer, has never yet been reached. A man will lie on his back in the harvest field, under a hedge sweet with the June roses that smile upon the hay, and never move or take his lips away till a gallon has entered into his being, for it can hardly be said to be swallowed. Two gallons a day is not an uncommon consumption with men who swing the scythe or reaping-hook.

This of course is small beer; but the stuff called for at the low public in the village, or by the road just outside, though indescribably nauseous to a non-vitiated palate, is not 'small.' It is a heady liquid, which if anyone drinks, not being accustomed to it, will leave its effects upon him

MELKSHAM

for hours afterwards. But this is what the labourer likes. He prefers something that he can feel; something that, if sufficiently indulged in, will make even his thick head spin and his temples ache next morning. Then he has had the value of his money.

*Richard Jefferies*

## TARPS

*Borough Police Court,* Tuesday, – Before Horace Cooper, esq. – *Joseph Dash* of Milton, locally known as 'Tarps' a drover, was brought up charged with having been drunk in the High Street on the previous evening. He pleaded guilty. P.C. Harrison stated that about half-past five on Monday night near the Bear and Castle, the prisoner was very drunk and using disgusting language. He requested him to go away several times, but defendant refused. Once he got him out of the town on his way home, but he returned, and the constable was obliged to lock him up. The police had had trouble with him several times before. He hit the constable when searching him at the police station in his face. The defendant pleaded hard for forgiveness, once going on his knees with his hands clasped and promising not to offend again. A fine of 2s. 6d. including costs, was imposed, defendant being allowed time in which to pay.

*Devizes and Wiltshire Gazette, 27 November 1890*

MARLBOROUGH

THE KEMM FAMILY, AVEBURY MANOR

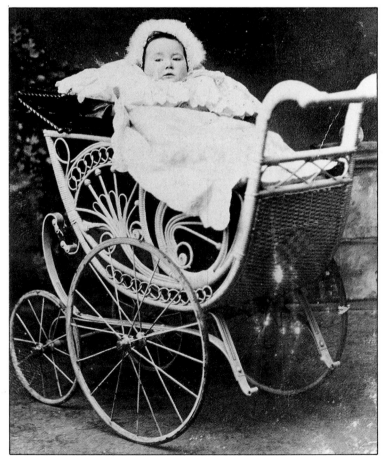

AVEBURY

## NURSERY TEA

The rocking-horse was exactly above the canopy of Granny's bed. She was quite often in bed when we all decided to go for a gallop. But she would sit there serenely in her white lace cap – which she never took off by day except to put on a hat – waiting for the screeching nursery floorboards to give way and the stunning impact of our combined arrival.

One day, when she knew that we had all gone out for a walk, she was astonished to hear the familiar creaking and pounding going on above her ceiling. Going up to the nursery to investigate, she found the nursery maid in full gallop. She was only fourteen, and had come from an orphanage. Her hair – although I cannot remember either it or her – was apparently so tightly skinned back from her forehead to her plait that she could not shut her eyes!

Nursery meals followed the same pattern whatever nursery they were eaten in – whether it was at the Close, or at home, or in some room doing duty as a nursery in a house by the sea. Given the amenities, these meals would have preserved their unswerving ritual – provided, of course, that Nanny was there – in the middle of the Sahara Desert. But tea in the Close nursery in the winter is the meal that I remember the best, with the kettle on the hob and the gently wheezing gas. The etiquette was as rigid as

SUNDAY SCHOOL TEA, BOWERCHALKE

that of an official dinner party. But, unlike the timorous young man who peeled his grapes with a knife, we knew our stuff even if we did not do it. Hands washed, hair tidied, we surrounded the table. Nanny kicked off with grace. *For what we are going to receive may the Lord make us truly thankful.* With folded hands and eyes shut – or not, according to our mood and the strength of our temptation – we accompanied her. We received bread and butter first. To receive anything else would have been as unthinkable as not putting on clean drawers on Sunday. Nor must the bread and butter be grabbed straight off the plate and crammed into our mouths. Good manners demanded that it should be laid for an appreciable moment on our own plates *en passant.* After that came bread and jam, or bread and honey. Never butter as well. The china honey-pot, made in the shape of a straw bee-hive, with a bee climbing up it, was of enduring interest. Cake came last – the peak to which we had munched our way, blunting the greedy edge of our appetites. *Always take the cake nearest to you.* This rule, of course, applied to everything, but cake was the thing that mattered. Heartbreak, to get a cake with two cherries in it, when the one behind had six! This led to intrigue, malice, and cheating. The boiled egg which I, as the puniest, was given, led to downright hatred.

'Why can't we have eggs?' said Ena whose name had long ago become shortened and Anglicized for workaday purposes.

'Because you don't need them,' said Nanny.

'*She* always has everything', said Sylvia.

'Now then, you know that's not true. Wipe your mouth.'

'I want an egg!' Helen's foot came down wang on the rung of her chair.

'Go and stand in the corner', said Nanny.

Sliding off her chair, Helen went proudly off on her fat legs. Nothing would induce her to show she minded. There was a little hole in the wall with the paper off. Presently, she started to pick it. . . .

*Geraldine Symons*

## DIARY

*Monday, 14 December*

This evening at 5 o'clock I took 21 of our schoolchildren into Chippenham to the Temperance Hall to see a Panorama of the African travels of Dr Livingstone. One of the most favourite pictures with the chilren was the Funeral of Dr Livingstone in Westminster Abbey. The Abbey was first shown empty. Then by a slight dioramic effect or dissolving view the open space in the Nave gradually melted into the forms of the funeral party, Dean Stanley

AVEBURY SCHOOL

reading the service and the mourners grouped round the flower wreath-covered coffin.

*Thursday, 17 December*
This morning after long suspense and waiting we were thankful to receive the happy news that dear Thersie was safely confined of a fine boy at Monnington Rectory at 10 p.m. Tuesday, 15th December. Thank God for this and all His mercies.

*Tuesday, 22 December*
Mrs John Knight tells me that the Malmesbury people are commonly called 'Jackdaws', to their intense disgust. It is a common saying among folks going to Malmesbury, 'Let us go and see the Malmesbury Jackdaws'. I remember hearing many years ago, I think among the people of Kington St Michael, that jackdaws are often called in these parts 'The Parsons from Malmesbury Abbey'. Perhaps the grey polls of the birds may have suggested the shaven polls of the monks, or the thievish habits of the jackdaws may have called to remembrance some tradition of the rapacity of the Abbot of Malmesbury.

*Thursday, Christmas Eve*
Writing Christmas letters all the morning. In the afternoon I went to the Church with Dora and Teddy to put up the Christmas decorations. Dora has been very busy for some days past making the straw letters for the Christmas text. Fair Rosamund and good Elizabeth Knight came to the Church to help us and worked heartily and well. They had made some pretty ivy knots and bunches for the pulpit panels and the ivy blossoms cleverly whitened with flour looked just like white flowers.

The churchwarden Jacob Knight was sitting by his sister in front of the roaring fire. We were talking of the death of Major Torrens on the ice at Corsham pond yesterday. Speaking of people slipping and falling on ice the good churchwarden sagely remarked, 'Some do fall on their faces and some do fall on their rumps. And they as do hold their selves uncommon stiff do most in generally fall on their rumps.'

*Francis Kilvert*

## SOLD BY AUCTION

The day is a dull and depressing one towards the end of winter, and, as everyone tells you, when the wind drops it will rain with a vengeance. The plain old farmhouse – every tile on whose once red roof has long since changed the original hue of its fiery youth for a separate tint of its own more befitting advanced age – has looked on the village green for a century or two; and though, probably,

CALNE

in its best days it never laid itself out to be particuarly joyful, to-day it looks gloomier than ever. Yet deceptive appearances would suggest to a stranger that it was having a specially good time. It stands a few yards back from the road which runs between it and the village green. A low wall with a wicket gate in the centre divides the garden from the road. Entering the gate, you go through the garden by a straight path to the front door. The door stands open, and men are hurrying in and out, in a free and easy fashion unsuited to its staid and formal demeanour. The barns are great rambling buildings, such as no one would think of putting up nowdays. To the right of them on one side is a large fold-yard, surrounded by cow-houses and cart-stables; and at the back of these is an imposing rick-yard, full of large but slovenly ricks of straw. To the left of the buildings is a paddock containing three or four acres; and on one side of this paddock is a vast array of agricultural implements of all sorts and ages, drawn up in a double row. Some of the implements, if old-fashioned, are useful enough; but you are struck by the evident fact that years must have passed since the stock welcomed a new arrival even of the least important and cheapest sort. There is absolutely nothing approaching to new, save here and there a patch of red paint on a cart-wheel, which has been hurriedly mended to enable it to scramble through the ordeal of the sale; indeed there is a great deal in the paddock that is very old. The student of past agricultural customs has here a rare opportunity of extending his knowledge. Ploughs enough are here of all dates, patterns, and materials, with the rust of long years

on their feeble and worn-out coulters. These typify so well the used-up agricultural labourer, that you are not in the least surprised to see him standing beside them in his old smock and leaning on two sticks. The sale is just beginning; and he shows his sympathy by accompanying with nods and smiles, each tardy bid evoked by the sanguine auctioneer. Were it not for his poverty-stricken appearance, half of the old implements would be knocked down to him. As each is sold he envies and mentally (sometimes audibly) congratulates the fortunate owner. Poor old fellow! Once he walked stoutly along between the stilts of the very plough for which someone has just bid 2*s*. 9*d*.

The loud monotonous bellow of the auctioneer's voice booms about you as you drive into the yard, and your horse is taken out by an old ostler from the 'Farmer's Arms', who attends to-day by special permission, as by long practice he can pack a hundred traps into a smaller compass than any other man for miles around. The majority of intending visitors have already arrived in all sorts and degrees of vehicles; from the smart new gig of the 'apron farmer', who has a shop in town and who is now a very rare bird indeed, to pig-dealers and scrap-iron higglers, whose crazy traps, picked up on some occasion like the present, rattle gaily along as if pleased with the prospect of almost immediate dissolution. A few heavy men are still descending with care from dealers' carts and walking into the house with their whips and wraps. They will emerge when the sheep and cattle are put up, and proceed to business with a depressed and ruminating air.

ESTATE STAFF, BOWOOD

Nobody who is known at all thinks of waiting to be asked into the house, where little hungry pig-jobbers are nervously working their eager elbows into the well-covered ribs of big farmers. The chair on these occasions is taken by the auctioneer until the hour for beginning business calls him away. The auctioneer is naturally the most hospitable of hosts; but in this respect he is almost equalled by the farmer, the hero of the day, who succeeds him. A farmer will cling desperately to hospitality while he has a spare crust left and a mug of sour cider. Looking through the lattice-panes of the small old-fashioned windows you get a misty glimpse of a long table, crowded with guests who are feeding against time, and most of them, sad to say, feeding with their knives. Some of these men have come a long way, and will return whence they came without having caught the auctioneer's roving eye. There are farmers, and impecunious ones too, who would never dream of missing a sale; and there is a general feeling that it is right and proper to attend the sale of the effects of a man you know, as if it were his funeral. In each district the same men are to be met at all sales. Hence the apparently wonderful knowledge possessed by auctioneers of all their customers' affairs.

As you enter the house, the farmer whose stock is being sold is just leaving for the sale ground. He looks happy enough, and not at all as if the home where he has lived for a great part of his life was being broken up. Poor fellow!

MARKET LAVINGTON

MARLBOROUGH

He doubtless feels that a great load of care and anxiety is being removed from shoulders which could not have borne it much longer. If he regrets anything, it is that he did not give up at the beginning of the bad times. But the auctioneer has now finished with the implements, and has ordered his rostrum (a wheelbarrow, from which he descends when he has disposed of articles in his immediate neighbourhood, to remount it a few yards further on) to be wheeled to the other side of the paddock. There he is going to sell the sheep, which are penned on a ridge of higher ground, five sheep in a pen. A dense crowd is here gathered together. The auctioneer has not hitherto driven a very thriving trade, but now he will do better. Hitherto his eloquence has been expended on objects which are not of universal desire.

There is but little difficulty in selling the sheep, though they do not bring the prices of former years. By-and-by the rostrum is wheeled by the attendant satellite up to a low wall which runs between the paddock and the farm-yard. The cows are one by one driven as close as possible to the auctioneer on the other side of the wall, through a dense crowd which opens out to let them pass and then closes up again. The 'company' stands about the yard in groups wherever there are no manure-heaps, and some-times where there are. When a frightened animal is in position, the assistant drovers work their sticks merrily to keep her in it. If she moves an inch she gets a rap from some quarter, and soon learns she had better stand still. As

you stand by the auctioneer you meet the curious spectacle of a hundred or two of faces looking steadfastly in the same direction, each wearing an exactly similar expres-sion. When the sale languishes, a jug of punch appears as if by magic and the biddings soon start again. The last lot is reached as the sun is going down. It is the old sheep-dog, a great local favourite, who is knocked down for a sovereign to a neighbour who will value him.

*Richard Jefferies*

## THE CARRIER'S CART

Apart from commerce, the carrier's covered brake was available to whoever wished to hire it. For example visits to gardens shows, fêtes and mission meetings in adjacent villages are mentioned. The rough roads could make the journey hazardous. On the way to Salisbury, while de-livering goods, Billie Williams was once thrown from the van sustaining very bad bruising to his arm and shoulder. A more serious accident occurred in 1900 as he was travelling across the steep downs to Handley. His horse fell suddenly cutting both knees so badly that it had to be shot. Such a disaster to a carrier was, of course, catastro-phic and it is much to the village's credit – as well as their own self-interest – that an ensuing collection raised suf-

SALISBURY

ficient money for him to purchase a new horse.

The Williams family ran their carrier service to the Chough Inn, Salisbury three times weekly. The journey was slow: Billie Williams would leave the village at 9.30 a.m. to arrive in Salisbury by 1 p.m. Stabling was provided at The Three Swans, and the cart would be left in procession with numerous others in Blue Boar Row. Fred Penny claims that although the waggon was always left unattended while Mr Williams went about his various commissions no parcel was ever stolen from it. The return journey commenced at 6 p.m., arriving home about 11 p.m. Billie Williams liked a drink and the slower journey home was due to his many pauses for refreshment at each of the valley taverns – often to the great annoyance of his passengers.

*Rex Sawyer*

## LUNCH

Towards the hour of noon Harry Hodson, of Upcourt Farm, was slowly ascending the long slope that led to his dwelling. In his left hand he carried a hare, which swung slightly to and fro as he stepped out, and the black-tipped ears rubbed now and then against a bunch of grass. His double-barrel was under his right arm. Every day at the same hour Harry turned towards home, for he adhered to the ways of his fathers and dined at half-past twelve,

except when the stress of harvest, or some important agricultural operation, disturbed the usual household arrangements. It was a beautiful October day, sunny and almost still, and, as he got on the high ground, he paused and looked round. The stubbles stretched far away on one side, where the country rose and fell in undulations. On the distant horizon a column of smoke, broadening at the top, lifted itself into the sky; he knew it was from the funnel of a steam-plough, whose furnace had just been replenished with coal. The appearance of the smoke somewhat resembled that left by a steamer at sea when the vessel is just below the horizon. On the other hand were wooded meadows, where the rooks were cawing – some on the oaks, some as they wheeled round in the air. Just beneath him stood a row of wheat ricks – his own. His gaze finally rested upon their conical roofs with satisfaction, and he then resumed his walk.

Even as he moved he seemed to bask in the sunshine; the sunshine pouring down from the sky above, the material sunshine of the goodly wheat ricks, and the physical sunshine of personal health and vigour. His walk was the walk of a strong, prosperous man – each step long, steady, and firm, but quite devoid of haste. He was, perhaps, forty years of age, in the very prime of life, and though stooping a little, like so many countrymen, very tall, and built proportionately broad across the shoulders and chest. His features were handsome – perhaps there was a trace of indolence in their good-humoured expression – and he had a thick black beard just marked with one thin wavy line of grey. That trace of snow, if anything, rather added to the

WARMINSTER

manliness of his aspect, and conveyed the impression that he was at the fulness of life when youth and experience meet. If anything, indeed, he looked too comfortable, too placid. A little ambition, a little restlessness, would perhaps have been good for him.

By degrees he got nearer to the house; but it was by degrees only, for he stayed to look over every gate, and up into almost every tree. He stopped to listen as his ear caught the sound of hoofs on the distant road, and again at the faint noise of a gun fired a mile away. At the corner of a field a team of horses – his own – were resting awhile as the carter and his lad ate their luncheon. Harry stayed to talk to the man, and yet again at the barn door to speak to his men at work within with the winnowing machine. The homestead stood on an eminence, but was hidden by elms and sycamores, so that it was possible to pass at a distance without observing it.

On entering the sitting-room Harry leaned his gun against the wall in the angle between it and the bureau, from which action alone it might have been known that he was a bachelor, and that there were no children about the house to get into danger with fire-arms. His elderly aunt,

who acted as house-keeper, was already at table waiting for him. It was spread with a snow-white cloth, and almost equally snow-white platter for bread – so much and so well was it cleaned. They ate home-baked bread; they were so many miles from a town or baker that it was difficult to get served regularly, a circumstance which preserved that wholesome institution. There was a chine of bacon, small ale, and a plentiful supply of good potatoes. The farmer did full justice to the sweet picking off the chine, and then lingered over an old cheese.

*Richard Jefferies*

## FACTORY PRANKS

One prank that used to be greatly in vogue in the shed was that of inserting a brick in the sleeve of a workmate's jack as it was hanging up underneath the wall or behind the forge. This was sometimes done for pure sport, though occasionally there was more than a spice of malice in the jest. Perhaps the owner of the garment had been guilty of

GWR FACTORY DINING ROOM, SWINDON

an offence, of tale-bearing, or something or other to the prejudice of his fellow-mates, and this was the means adopted for his punishment. Accordingly, a large brick was quietly dropped into the sleeve from inside the shoulder and well shaken down to the cuff, and the jacket was left hanging innocently in its position. At hooter time all those in the secret congregated and waited for the victim of the joke to come for his coat. Suddenly, as the hooter sounded, he rushed up in a great hurry, seized his coat and discovered the impediment, while all the others speedily decamped. He had considerable difficulty in dislodging the brick from the sleeve. After trying in vain for ten minutes or more he was usually forced to cut away the sleeve, or the lining, with his pocket-knife.

Another favourite trick was to place some kind of seat under a wall in order to entice the unwary, and to fix up above it a large tin full of soot, so arranged as to work on a pivot, and operated by means of a string. The soot was also sometimes mixed with water, and stirred up so as to make an intensely black fluid. By and by an unsuspecting workman – usually an interloper from the yard or else-where – would come along and sit down upon the improvised seat. Very soon one of the gang shouted out 'Hey up!' sharply, and as the victim jumped up someone pulled the string and down came soot, water, and very often the pot, too, upon his head. If the joke was successful the dupe's face was as black as a sweep's; a loud roar of laughter went up from the workmen and the unhappy victim very quickly got outside. Sometimes, however, he did not take it so quietly, and I have seen a free fight as the outcome of this adventure.

*Alfred Williams*

PURTON

REGENT CIRCUS, SWINDON

## COOLING OFF

The toilers have resort to various methods in order to mitigate the heat during the summer months. The fur- nacemen, stampers, and forgers usually remove their shirts altogether, and discard their leathern aprons for those made of light canvas, or old rivet bags. The amount of cold water drunk at such times is enormous. It is useless to advise the men to take it in moderation: 'I don't care, I must have it,' is the answer made. Occasionally the officials issue oatmeal from the stores, to be taken with the water. This removes the rawness from the liquid, and makes it much more palatable, and less harmful to the stomach. The boys are especially fond of the mixture; they would drink it by the bucketful, and swallow grouts and all. They do not believe in wasting anything obtained gratis from the company.

One plan, in very hot weather, is to wrap a wet towel or wiper about the head, cooling it now and then with fresh water. Some hold their heads and faces underneath the tap and let the cool water run upon them; and others engage their mates to squirt it in their faces instead. Such as do this

tie an apron close around the neck under the chin, and receive the volume of water full in the face. It is delicious, when you are baked and half-choked with the heat in midsummer, to go to the big tap under the wall and receive the cold water on the inside part of the arm, just below the shoulder, allowing it to run down and flow off the finger tips. This is very cooling and refreshing, and is a certain restorative.

Now and then, during the meal-hour, a hardy workman will strip himself and bathe in the big bosh used for cooling the furnace tools. In the evening, after a hard sweating at the fires, many of the young men will pay a visit to the baths in the town. Little Jim and his mates, who have no coppers to squander upon the luxury of a dip under cover, betake themselves to the clay-pits in a neighbouring brick-field. There they dive down among the fishes and forget about the punishment they have suffered today, and which is certainly awaiting them on the morrow.

*Alfred Williams*

TRIP DAY, SWINDON

## TRIP DAY

'Trip Day' is the most important day in the calendar at the railway town. For several months preceding it, fathers and mothers of families, young unmarried men, and juveniles have been saving up for the outing. Whatever new clothes are bought for the summer are usually worn for the first time at 'Trip'; the trade of the town is at its zenith during the week before the holiday. Then the men don their new suits of shoddy, and the pinched or portly dames deck themselves out in all the glory of cheap, 'fashionable' finery. The young girls are radiant with colour – white, red, pink, and blue – and the children come dressed in brand-new garments – all stiff from the warehouse – and equipped with spade and bucket and bags full of thin paper, cut the size of pennies, to throw out of the carriage windows as the train flies along. A general exodus from the town takes place that day and quite twenty-five thousand people will have been hurried off to all parts of the kingdom in the early hours of the morning, before the ordinary traffic begins to get thick on the line. About half the total number return the same night; the others stop away till the expiration of the holiday, which is of eight days' duration.

The privilege of travelling free by the Trip trains is not granted to all workmen, but only to those who are

TRIP DAY POSTCARD

71

GWR CHILDREN'S FETE

members of the local Railway Institute and Library, and have contributed about six shillings per annum to the general fund. Moreover, no part of the holiday is free, but is counted as lost time. The prompt commencement of work after Trip is, therefore, highly necessary; the great majority of the workmen are reduced to a state of absolute penury. If they have been away and spent all their money – and perhaps incurred debt at home for rent and provisions beforehand in order to enjoy themselves the better on their trip – it will take them a considerable time to get square again; they will scarcely have done this before the Christmas holidays are announced.

At the end of the first week after the Trip holiday there will be no money to draw. When Friday comes round, bringing with it the usual hour for receiving the weekly wages, the men file out of the sheds with long faces. This is generally known at the works as 'The Grand March Past,' because the toilers march past the pay-table and receive nothing that day. The living among the poorest of the workmen will be very meagre, and a great many will not have enough to eat until the next Friday comes round, bringing with it the first pay. The local tradesmen and shopkeepers look upon the Trip as a great nuisance because, they say, it takes money away from the town that ought to be spent in their warehouses; they do not take into consideration the fact that the men are confined like

prisoners all the rest of the year.

Work in the sheds, for the first day or two after the Trip, goes very hard and painful; everyone is yearning towards the blue sea or the fresh open country, and thinking of friends and kindred left beind. This feeling very soon wears off, however. Long before the week is over the spirit of work will have taken possession of the men; they fall naturally into their places and the Trip becomes a thing of the past – a dream and a memory. Here and there you may see scrawled upon the wall somewhere or other, with a touch of humour, '51 weeks to Trip'; that is usually the last word in connection with it for another year.

*Alfred Williams*

## HELP FROM THE SHEPHERD

When we were carrying corn the number of pitchers in the field loading the wagons, and the number of men at the rick emptying them, had to be regulated to a nicety to keep the wagons going backwards and forwards steadily without a hitch. That is where Tommy and the trap came in. Tommy would be required earlier during the harvest; as a matter of fact he stayed harnessed to the trap all day

LUDGERSHALL

until knock-off time. The wagons were led from the field to the rick and back by small boys. One of my father's dictums was that two boys together did half as much as one boy by himself, and that three boys did nothing at all. Let two of the boys stop for a minute or two as they passed, one with a full wagon and the other with an empty one, and the whole business of carrying was disorganized. Then, from some point of vantage, Tommy and the trap descended on them like the wrath of God. On these urgent occasions Thomas moved quite smartly.

I can appreciate now that my father's work in this way was very important. He would also play off the rick staff against the field men. Perhaps we would be a pitcher short of the required number owing to one of the carters having gone to the station for a load of something. Father would drive out to the other pitchers, and say to the head carter: ''Fraid you won't be able to keep us going so well to-day till Fred gets back. Still, we must put up with it. Just do the best you can.' Or perhaps the rick staff would be a man or two short for a similar reason, and it would be: 'I wonder if I'd better drive down to the dairy, and see if a milker can be spared for a bit. You chaps won't keep those pitchers going else.' 'Doan' 'ee worry, zur,' they would be sure to say, 'we'll manage somehow.'

If the occasion were desperate, and another hand must be got somehow, the shepherd was the last resort. You didn't send the foreman to see if the shepherd could get away for an hour or two. That would have been to court disaster. The sheep would have been in such a critical state that if the shepherd left for a moment, they would all be sure to die. Neither was I sent. Youth hadn't the tact required for such a ticklish operation. Oh no! That was a job for the Guvnor, and from the rick we would see Tommy being urged to his most furious speed up the far slope towards the sheepfold. Having arrived, my father talked sheep, sheep, and nothing but sheep, thus relegating the harvest to an unimportant detail unworthy of mention. After a bit the shepherd would be sure to say: 'And how be getten on wi' the carrying, zur?' 'Pretty fair, shepherd. We're a bit shorthanded today. I'm on my way down to the village to see if I can pick up another man.' 'Well, zur, I be about straight yer just now, in a manner o' speaking. Ud it be any good if I were to gie 'ee a hand fer an hour or two?' And back to the harvest field would come Tommy, hauling both the shepherd and my father, who had achieved his object without mentioning it.

*A.G. Street*

73

FISHERTON DE LA MERE

WROUGHTON

## THE CONGREGATION

It is interesting to enter the church early, and see the worshippers come in, the old men first, afterwards the youths and maidens, and finally the children. Robert Brooks was a regular attendant at morning service, though over eighty-five; he is in the workhouse now. His grey beard and shaking head, as he walked feebly up the nave, were pathetic to see; his was a striking figure. Next came William Maisey, hard on four score. He wore heavy nailed boots, and gaiters of corduroy, with both hands held down by his sides. His old head was frosty white, and his short beard the same; his nose was prominent, his eyes kindly, his whole expression exceedingly pleasant. His heavy boots sounded loud on the paved floor; he cloutered along noisily, but he was welcome; everyone had a smile and a kind word for old William; and one young married woman took such a fancy to him that she went up to him and kissed him outright.

The village maidens are delightful to see. There is a town and a country beauty; the former is cultivated and derived, the latter is natural born, as artless and fresh and lovable as the wild roses that bloom about the fields in early summer.

The dress of the country maidens, too, where they have not been too much influenced by the town styles, is simpler, more tasteful and suitable, more becoming and natural. There is little pretence to elaborate finery. In the summer you see whites and creams, in the winter warm reds and blues. In the sunny days the cool thin muslin and large-brimmed straw hat. There is another quality which agrees so well with beauty in the village maidens, that is, demureness; they are not self-conscious. This is bred of rusticity, of simple life and conversation, of innocency, and is the most lovable feature of all, though it is rarer now than it used to be.

The little boys and girls march in all together, the boys cap in hand, cloutering along with heavy boots, panting and sweating very often, for they have been playing in the field, likely enough, and are very nearly exhausted. The girls walk quietly round to the transept, leading little Jacky or Tommy by the hand, who turns his head over his shoulder and looks behind him all the way with wide open eyes, astonished to see so many people together. The poor mother enters with her little swarm, and places them all along in the seat beside her, and hands them books, as many as can tell the words and letters.

The sermon in the village church is often long, and the minister severe. Knowing all his flock so nearly and well, he is pretty much acquainted with their several weaknesses and shortcomings; and when anything of note transpires – if this one is guilty of some little fault or indiscretion, or that one has been 'having it over' with his neighbour, or has been absent from his pew for a long time, and so on – some kind of reference to it will most certainly be made; everyone in the building regards the allusion, and recognizes the person for whom it is intended. There is a good deal of nudging in the pews.

*Alfred Williams*

WARMINSTER

## GOSSIPS

For golden opportunities for gossip, what can surpass the Carriers cart? It goes so slowly to and from the market town; under its black hood the gossips are so snug and secure from interruption, from eaves dropping. The establishments of squire and parson, the doings of neighbour this and neighbour that, up street and down street – these are all overhauled in the Carriers cart. The ride to the market town in his vehicle is undoubtedly a treat – a distinct outing; and the shilling there and back is not high considering the distance and the hills. In some cases the hills are so steep that the heavier folk get out and walk, and the horse is made to take a winding course and now and then there is a short rest when a stone is put behind the back wheels to ease the poor beast; but on the level the Carriers cart attains to a jog trot when the burden is light.

*Edward Collett*

CARRIER'S CART, BOWERCHALKE

SALISBURY

## MARKET DAY

The doorway of the Jason Inn at Woolbury had nothing particular to distinguish it from the other doorways of the same extremely narrow street. There was no porch, nor could there possibly be one, for an ordinary porch would reach half across the roadway. There were no steps to go up, there was no entrance hall, no space specially provided for crowds of visitors; simply nothing but an ordinary street door opening directly on the street, and very little, if any, broader or higher than those of the private houses adjacent. There was not even the usual covered way or archway leading into the courtyard behind, so often found at old country inns; the approach to the stables and coach-houses was through a separate and even more narrow and winding street, necessitating a detour of some quarter of a mile. The dead, dull wall was worn smooth in places by the involuntary rubbings it had received from the shoulders of foot-passengers thrust rudely against it as the market-people came pouring in or out, or both together.

The pavement in front of the inn was barely eighteen inches wide; two persons could not pass each other on it, nor walk abreast. If a cart came along the roadway, and a trap had to go by it, the foot-passengers had to squeeze up against the wall, lest the box of the wheel projecting over the kerb shuld push them down. If a great waggon came loaded with wool, the chances were whether a carriage could pass it or not; as for a waggon-load of straw that projected from the sides, nothing could get by, but all must wait – till the huge mass had rumbled and jolted into the more open market-place.

But hard, indeed, must have been the flag-stones to withstand the wear and tear of the endless iron-shod shoes that tramped to and fro these mere ribbons of pavements. For, besides the through traffic out from the market-place to the broad macadamised road that had taken the place and the route of an ancient Roman road, there were the customers to the shops that lined each side of the street. Into some of these you stepped from the pavement down, as it were, into a cave, the level of the shop being eight or ten inches below the street, while the first floor projected over the pavement quite to the edge of the kerb. To enter these shops it was necessary to stoop, and when you were inside there was barely room to turn round. Other shops were, indeed, level with the street; but you had to be careful, because the threshold was not flush with the pavement, but rose a couple of inches and then fell again, a

TROWBRIDGE

very trap to the toe of the unwary. Many had no glass at all, but were open, like a butcher's or fishmonger's. Those that had glass were so restricted for space that, rich as they might be within in the good things of the earth, they could make no 'display.' All the genius of a West-end shopman could not have made an artistic arrangement in that narrow space and in that bad light; for, though so small below, the houses rose high, and the street being so narrow the sunshine rarely penetrated into it.

But mean as a metropolitan shopman might have thought the spot, the business done there was large, and, more than that, it was genuine. The trade of a country market-town, especially when that market-town, like Woolbury, dates from the earliest days of English history, is hereditary. It flows to the same store and to the same shop year after year, generation after generation, century after century. The farmer who walks into the saddler's here goes in because his father went there before him. His father went in because his father dealt there, and so on farther back than memory can trace. It might almost be said that whole villages go to particular shops.

On a market-day like this there is, of course, the incessant entry and exit of carts, waggons, traps, gigs, four-wheels, and a large number of private carriages. The number of private carriages is, indeed, very remarkable, as also the succession of gentlemen on thoroughbred horses – a proof of the number of resident gentry in the neighbour-

hood, and of its general prosperity. Cart-horses furbished up for sale, with straw-bound tails and glistening skins; 'baaing' flocks of sheep; squeaking pigs; bullocks with their heads held ominously low, some going, some returning, from the auction yard; shouting drovers; lads rushing hither and thither; dogs barking; everything and everybody crushing, jostling, pushing through the narrow street. An old shepherd, who has done his master's business, comes along the pavement, trudging thoughtful and slow, with ashen staff. One hand is in his pocket, the elbow of the arm projecting; he is feeling a fourpenny-piece, and deliberating at which 'tap' he shall spend it. He fills up the entire pavement, and stolidly plods on, turning ladies and all into the roadway; not from intentional rudeness, but from sheer inability to perceive that he is causing inconvenience.

Unless you know the exact spot it is difficult in all this crowd and pushing, with a nervous dread of being gored from behind by a bull, or thrown off your feet by a sudden charge of sheep, to discover the door of the Jason Inn. That door has been open every legitimate and lawful hour this hundred years; but you will very likely be carried past it and have to struggle back. Then it is not easy to enter, for half a dozen stalwart farmers and farmers' sons are coming out; while two young fellows stand just inside, close to the sliding bar-window, blocking up the passage, to exchange occasional nods and smiles with the barmaid.

CRICKLADE

However, by degrees you shuffle along the sanded passage, and past the door of the bar, which is full of farmers as thick as they can stand, or sit. The rattle of glasses, the chink of spoons, the hum of voices, the stamping of feet, the calls and orders, and sounds of laughter, mingle in confusion. Cigar-smoke and the steam from the glasses fill the room – with a thick white mist, through which rubicund faces dimly shine like the red sun through a fog.

Some at the table are struggling to write cheques, with continual jogs at the elbow, with ink that will not flow, pens that scratch and splutter, blotting-paper that smudges and blots. Some are examining cards of an auction, and discussing the prices which they have marked in the margin in pencil. The good-humoured uproar is beyond description, and is increased by more farmers forcing their way in from the rear, where are their horses or traps – by farmers eagerly inquiring for dealers or friends, and by messengers from the shops loaded with parcels to place in the customer's vehicle.

*Richard Jefferies*

## THE VANISHING CURTSEY

I was walking in the village street with a lady friend when we noticed four little girls coming towards us with arms linked. As they came near they suddenly stopped and

curtseyed all together in an exaggerated manner, dropping till their knees touched the ground, then springing to their feet they walked rapidly away. From the bold, free, easy way in which the thing was done it was plain to see that they had been practising the art in something of a histrionic spirit for the benefit of the pilgrims and strangers frequently seen in the village, and for their own amusement. As the little Selbornians walked off they glanced back at us over their shoulders, exhibiting four roguish smiles on their four faces. The incident greatly amused us, but I am not sure that the Reverend Gilbert White would have regarded it in the same humorous light.

Occasionally one even finds a village where strangers are not often seen, which has yet outlived the curtsey. Such a place, I take it, is Alvediston, the small downland village on the upper waters of the Ebble, in southern Wiltshire. One day last summer I was loitering near the churchyard, when a little girl, aged about eight, came from an adjoining copse with some wild flowers in her hand. She was singing as she walked and looked admiringly at the flowers she carried; but she could see me watching her out of the corners of her eyes.

'Good morning,' said I. 'It is nice to be out gathering flowers on such a day, but why are you not in school?'

'Why am I not in school?' in a tone of surprise. 'Because the holidays are not over. On Monday we open.'

'How delighted you will be.'

'Oh no, I don't *think* I shall be delighted,' she returned. Then I asked her for a flower, and apparently much

BLACKLANDS MILL, CALNE

amused she presented me with a water forget-me-not, then she sauntered on to a small cottage close by. Arrived there, she turned round and faced me, her hand on the gate, and after gazing steadily for some moments exclaimed, 'Delighted at going back to school – who ever heard such a thing?' and, bursting into a peal of musical child-laughter, she went into the cottage.

One would look for curtseys in the Flower Walk in Kensington Gardens as soon as in the hamlet of this remarkably self-possessed little maid. Her manner was exceptional; but, if we must lose the curtsey, and the rural little ones cease to mimic that pretty drooping motion of the nightingale, the kitty wren, and wheatear, cannot our village pastors and masters teach them some less startling and offensive form of salutation than the loud'Hullo!' with which they are accustomed to greet the stranger within their gates!

*W.H. Hudson*

## PATSY, THE WATERCRESS MAN

In the spring and early summer there is an abundance of large watercress growing in the stream, and about the trenches of the meadows as well. The boys and men from the farms know where to find this; almost any Sunday morning you may meet one or other of them bearing a bundle tied up in a red pocket-handkerchief.

Years ago there were professional watercress men, but these are not so much in evidence here lately, since old 'Patsy' died. Patsy was a familiar figure about the village, and in the town too. He had been the local watercress man for many years, and had grown old in the occupation; he was well over seventy when he was forced to retire from it. Patsy was short and slight in stature, bent and stooping; his clothes were ragged and rough, his coat-sleeves long, and his trousers short; his boots were very old, and full of holes; his feet were naked within them; his hair was long and grey; his weather-beaten old face was clean shaved and

HIGHWORTH

sharpish looking. He wore an old cloth cap, and carried a large flat-shaped open basket at his back, slung with cord over the shoulders. As a rule, he was only visible in the mornings and evenings; during the daytime he was lost in the far-off fields, and about the brooks and ditches. When he had obtained a sufficient quantity of cresses, he used to take them to the town and dispose of them to the small shopkeepers, and so eke out a precarious living. At night he slept in the fields, under a haystack, or in the cattle-stalls, during the greater part of the year; in the dead of winter, he was forced to take refuge in the workhouse. He was well known to all and sundry round about, though he was very reserved in manner, and seldom conversed with people. His general conduct was above suspicion; he was trusted by all, and was never known to interfere with any; he was a lonely and solitary creature. The last time I saw him was one morning in late October some fifteen years ago. As I was passing through the town on my way to work at an early hour I saw Patsy standing underneath the wall of a house on the pavement, in a most abject

condition. The morning was cold and raw; there was frost in the air and some fog. He had his basket at his back, as usual, with a few cresses, and his old hands were thrust deep into his trousers pockets. His neck was open and bare; his feet and legs were very wet. I could tell by the mud on his boots where he had been. He was shivering with the cold; it was enough to give a stronger man than he his death. I can still see the crowd of workmen staring contemptuously upon him as they passed along, smug and comfortable enough, to the warm workshops. I can even now feel the hot blood mount up, as it did then, in indignation and sympathy for the old man. I loved him then for his utter abjectness, and because he knew and had frequented all those little nooks and crannies in the meadows I took such delight in. I never saw Patsy after that morning. I think he went to the workhouse, and soon after died there. His was a hard life, in some respects, and a cruel ending, but he loved the brooks and the fields.

*Alfred Williams*

EDINGTON CHURCH

## AUTUMN

This morning between breakfast and luncheon I walked up to Bowood to see the beeches by way of the Cradle Bridge, Tytherton Stanley and Studley Hill. I went into Bowood Park by the Studley Gate and turned sharp to the left down a drive that brought me soon into the very heart and splendour of the beeches. As the sun shone through the roof of beech boughs overhead the very air seemed gold and scarlet and green and crimson in the deep places of the wood and the red leaves shone brilliant standing out against the splendid blue of the sky. A crowd of wood pigeons rose from the green and misty azure hollows of the plantation and flapped swiftly down the glades, the blue light glancing off their clapping wings. I went by the house down to the lakeside and crossed the water by the hatches above the cascade. From the other side of the water the lake shone as blue as the sky and beyond it rose from the water's edge the grand bank of sloping woods glowing with colours, scarlet, gold, orange and crimson and dark green. Two men were fishing on the further shore of an arm of the lake and across the water came the hoarse belling of a buck while a coot fluttered skimming along the surface of the lake with a loud cry and rippling splash.

To eye and ear it was a beautiful picture, the strange hoarse belling of the buck, the fluttering of the coot as she skimmed the water with her melancholy note, the cry of the swans across the lake, the clicking of the reels as the fishermen wound up or let out their lines, the soft murmur

LORD AND LADY LANSDOWNE, BOWOOD

SPYE PARK, BOWDEN HILL

of the woods, the quiet rustle of the red and golden drifts of beech leaves, the rush of the waterfall, the light tread of the dappled herd of deer dark and dim glancing across the green glades from shadow into sunlight and rustling under the beeches, and the merry voices of the Marquis's children at play.

*Francis Kilvert*

## COUNTRY HOUSE

Certainly in the early Victorian period the middle classes expected the aristocracy to live luxuriously, and at times castigated them for it. Only towards the end of the century does one sense a growing attitude that comfort (and the new techniques that went with it) is *nouveau-riche*, unhealthy, or, even worse, American. Lord Ernest Hamilton

says that electric light was considered insufferably vulgar in its early days, and that the bathrooms of his country house boyhood were 'never used for the purposes for which they were no doubt originally designed'. Augustus Hare, in his interminable country house peregrinations, uses the word 'luxurious' almost exclusively for the houses of the new rich. Hutton Hall (home of the Middlesbrough Peases) is 'this intensely luxurious house'; the Guinness Elveden is 'almost appallingly luxurious'. Worst of all were the Montefiores at Worth Park, who had the presumption to make their servants comfortable as well as themselves: 'I went to Worth, the ultra-luxurious house of the Montefiores, where the servants have their own billiard tables, ballroom, theatre and pianofortes, and are arrogant and presumptuous in proportion.'

*Mark Girouard*

83

WESTBURY WHITE HORSE

## SHEEP-FOLD

The time to live is in the first few hours after dawn. There is an unearthly beauty and splendour abroad then, a magic spell over everything; the poetry and romance vanish under the glaring light of day. The evening is another matter. That is delightful, but the dawn is ecstatic.

There is a broad avenue of elms up the highway, too. Here you climb another slope, then come to a cross-roads: straight on to Hangman's Elm and Highworth, to the right Coleshill, to the left Sennington. The wonderful elms continue. This morning is a sharp frost. Close in the field is a sheep-fold, barricaded all round with thick walls of warm straw, and divided into numerous sections and compartments like a little city, for it will soon be lambing-time; and this is the shepherd coming with his dog. The old man is of average height, robust and healthy in appearance, tanned with the sun and the wind, with a fine nose, regular features, and most kind expression. His top lip is clean-shaven, he wears a grey beard under the chin, his frosty old brow is topped with a billy-cock hat, well soiled; he agrees well with the hoar frost on the grass and the rime on the branches. He wears a strong brown holland smock, well patched-up, heavy nailed boots, and thick leathern gaiters. In his hand he carries a stout staff with an iron crook at one end. He is not an Arcadian, and consequently lacks the pipe. He is rather a shepherd of real life; his flock is of best English ewes, tegs, and wethers.

His dog is a large, stocky animal, black and white, very old-fashioned-looking. He walks behind his master most respectfully, and observes a moderate distance. When you address the old man, he does not thrust himself into your notice, but stands or sits some way off, and looks sagely at you, or turns his head towards the fold. Doubtless he is thinking of the flock, and where he shall lead them to-morrow – among the swedes there or along the clover patch.

The old shepherd is pleased to speak to you. 'Yes, 'tis cowld; but a nice marnin, a know. Chent so cowld as 'twas.' He has been up a long time, and is off home to breakfast now. He is getting ready for the lambs. Will the cold hurt *them*? 'Bless ee, no, 's long as 'tis dry. Don matter 'ow cowld 'tis, 's long as chent wet; tha do get the rot so, then.' The iron crook looks cruel and out of place. 'Do you not hurt the poor sheep with it?' 'No, bless ee, not if ee be keerful. Some people do say as 'ow it do, and 'ow it breaks their legs, but I never hurted one in mi life, as I knows on. A okkerd fella might do 't, a know.' How sweet the baby lambs look when they are first born! They lie in a little nest made for them, and are nearly all ears and legs. Their pretty little noses and eyes are very quaint; when they are lying down they are like little figures in china or porcelain. The shepherd used to receive a bounty for lambs, but not now; that is included in his wages. On the downs there are sometimes as many as a thousand ewes, and these yield on an average eleven hundred lambs;

MILKING TEAM

but Shepherd Smith's flock is not nearly as big as that. A shepherd with a large flock of ewes is possessed of considerable skill, knowledge, and feeling too. See the life in his hands! He is father of a large family; he is physician, nurse, and guardian combined; he is the Providence of the fold. He is sometimes the Nemesis as well, for he must perforce play the butcher from time to time, and supply the house with mutton; he can kill and dress a sheep with the best of them.

*Alfred Williams*

## CITY MILK

There is a low murmur rather than a buzz along the hedgerow; but over it the hot summer breeze brings the thumping, rattling, booming sound of hollow metal striking against the ground or in contact with other metal. These ringing noises, which so little accord with the sweet-scented hay and green hedgerows, are caused by the careless handling of milk tins dragged hither and thither by the men who are getting the afternoon milk ready for transit to the railway station miles away. Each tin bears a brazen badge engraved with the name of the milkman who

will retail its contents in distant London. It may be delivered to the countess in Belgravia, and reach her dainty lip in the morning chocolate, or it may be eagerly swallowed up by the half-starved children of some back court in the purlieus of the Seven Dials.

Sturdy milkmaids may still be seen in London, sweeping the crowded pavement clear before them as they walk with swinging tread, a yoke on their shoulders, from door to door. Some remnant of the traditional dairy thus survives in the stony streets that are separated so widely from the country. But here, beside the hay, the hedgerows, the bees, the flowers that precede the blackberries – here in the heart of the meadows the romance has departed. Everything is mechanical or scientific. From the refrigerator that cools the milk, the thermometer that tests its temperature, the lactometer that proves its quality, all is mechanical precision. The tins themselves are metal – wood, the old country material for almost every purpose, is eschewed – and they are swung up into a waggon specially built for the purpose. It is the very antithesis of the jolting and cumbrous waggon used for generations in the hay-fields and among the corn. It is light, elegantly proportioned, painted, varnished – the work rather of a coachbuilder than a cartwright. The horse harnessed in it is equally unlike the cart-horse. a quick,

POTTERNE

wiry horse, that may be driven in a trap or gig, is the style – one that will rattle along and catch the train.

The driver takes his seat and handles the reins with the air of a man driving a tradesman's van, instead of walking, like the true old carter, or sitting on the shaft. The vehicle rattles off to the station, where ten, fifteen, or perhaps twenty such converge at the same hour, and then ensues a scene of bustle, chaff, and rough language. The tins are placed in the van specially reserved for them, the whistle sounds, the passengers – who have been wondering why on earth there was all this noise and delay at a little roadside station without so much as a visible steeple – withdraw their heads from the windows; the wheels revolve, and, gathering speed, the train disappears round the curve, hastening to the metropolis. Then the empty tins returned from town have to be conveyed home with more rattling, thumping, and booming of hollow tin.

*Richard Jefferies*

## DEER STEALERS

About this time some of the more ardent spirits in the village, not satisfied with an occasional hunt when a deer broke out and roamed over the downs, took to poaching them in the woods. One night, a hunt having been arranged, one of the most daring of the men secreted himself close to the keeper's house, and having watched the keepers go in and the lights put out, he actually succeeded in fastening up the doors from the outside with screws and pieces of wood without creating an alarm. He then met his confederates at an agreed spot and the hunting began, during which one deer was chased to the house and actually pulled down and killed on the lawn.

Meanwhile the inmates were in a state of great excitement; the under-keepers feared that a force it would be dangerous to oppose had taken possession of the woods, while Harbutt raved and roared like a maddened wild beast in a cage, and put forth all his strength to pull the doors open. Finally he smashed a window and leaped out, gun in hand, and calling the others to follow rushed into the wood. But he was too late; the hunt was over and the poachers had made good their escape, taking the carcasses of two or three deer they had succeeded in killing.

The keeper was not to be fooled in the same way a second time, and before very long he had his revenge. A fresh raid was planned, and on this occasion two of the five brothers were in it, and there were four more, the blacksmith of Winterbourne Bishop, their best man, two famous shearers, father and son, from a neighbouring village, and a young farm-labourer.

GASTARD

They knew very well that with the head-keeper in his present frame of mind it was a risky affair, and they made a solemn compact that if caught they would stand by one another to the end. And caught they were, and on this occasion the keepers were four.

At the very beginning the blacksmith, their ablest man and virtual leader, was knocked down senseless with a blow on his head with the butt end of a gun. Immediately on seeing this the two famous shearers took to their heels and the young labourer followed their example. The brothers were left but refused to be taken, although Harbutt roared at them in his bull's voice that he would shoot them unless they surrendered. They made light of his threats and fought against the four, and eventually were separated. By and by the younger of the two was driven into a brambly thicket where his opponents imagined that it would be impossible for him to escape. But he was a youth of indomitable spirit, strong and agile as a wild cat; and returning blow for blow he succeeded in tearing himself from them, then after a running fight through the darkest part of the wood for a distance of two or three hundred yards they at length lost him or gave him up and went back to assist Harbutt and Moses against the other man. Left to himself he got out of the wood and

made his way back to the village. It was long past midnight when he turned up at his father's cottage, a pitiable object covered with mud and blood, hatless, his clothes torn to shreds, his face and whole body covered with bruises and bleeding wounds.

The old man was in a great state of distress about his other son, and early in the morning went to examine the ground where the fight had been. It was only too easily found; the sod was trampled down and branches broken as though a score of men had been engaged. Then he found the eldest son's cap, and a little further away a sleeve of his coat; shreds and rags were numerous on the bramble bushes, and by and by he came on a pool of blood. 'They've kill 'en!' he cried in despair, 'they've killed my poor boy!' and straight to Rollston House he went to inquire, and was met by Harbutt himself, who came out limping, one boot on, the other foot bound up with rags, one arm in a sling and a cloth tied round his head. He was told that his son was alive and safe indoors and that he would be taken to Salisbury later in the day. 'His clothes be all torn to pieces,' added the keeper. 'You can just go home at once and git him others before the constable comes to take him.'

'You've tored them to pieces yourself and you can git

him others, 'retorted the old man in a rage.

'Very well,' said the keeper. 'But bide a moment – I've something more to say to you. When your son comes out of jail in a year or so you tell him from me that if he'll just step up this way I'll give him five shillings and as much beer as he lies to drink. I never see'd a better fighter!'

It was a great compliment to his son, but the old man was troubled in his mind. 'What dost mean, keeper, by a year or so?' he asked.

'When I said that,' returned the other, with a grin, 'I was just thinking what 'twould be he deserves to git.'

'And you'd agot your deserts, by God,' cried the angry father, 'if that boy of mine hadn't a-been left alone to fight ye!'

Harbutt regarded him with a smile of gratified malice. 'You can go home now,' he said. 'If you'd see your son you'll find'n in Salisbury jail. Maybe you'll be wanting new locks on your doors; you can git they in Salisbury too – you've no blacksmith in your village now. No, your boy weren't alone and you know that damned well.'

'I knew naught about that,' he returned, and started to walk home with a heavy heart. Until now he had been clinging to the hope that the other son had not been identified in the dark wood. And now what could he do to save one of the two from hateful imprisonment? The boy was not in a fit condition to make his escape; he could hardly get across the room and could not sit or lie down without groaning. He could only try to hide him in the cottage and pray that they would not discover him. The cottage was in the middle of the village and had but little ground to it, but there was a small, boarded-up cavity or cell at one end of an attic, and it might be possible to save him by putting him in there. Here, then, in a bed placed for him on the floor, his bruised son was obliged to lie, in the close, dark hole, for some days.

One day, about a week later, when he was recovering from his hurts, he crawled out of his box and climbed down the narrow stairs to the ground floor to see the light and breathe a better air for a short time, had while down he was tempted to take a peep at the street through the

CHIPPENHAM

small, latticed window. But he quickly withdrew his head and by and by said to his father, 'I'm feared Moses has seen me. Just now when I was at the window he came by and looked up and see'd me with my head all tied up, and I'm feared he knew 'twas I.'

After that they could only wait in fear and trembling, and on the next day quite early there came a loud rap at the door, and on its being opened by the old man the constable and two keepers appeared standing before him.

'I've come to take your son,' said the constable.

The old man stepped back without a word and took down his gun from its place on the wall, then spoke:

'If you've got a search-warrant you may come in; if you haven't got 'n I'll blow the brains out of the first man that puts a foot inside my door.'

They hesitated a few moments then silently withdrew. After consulting together the constable went off to the nearest magistrate, leaving the two keepers to keep watch on the house: Moses Found was one of them. Later in the day the constable returned armed with a warrant and was thereupon admitted, with the result that the poor youth was soon discovered in his hiding-place and carried off. And that was the last he saw of his home, his young sister crying bitterly and his old father white and trembling with grief and impotent rage.

A month or two later the two brothers were tried and sentenced to six months' imprisonment. They never came home. On their release they went to Woolwich, where men were wanted and the pay was good.

*W.H. Hudson*

TOWN CRIER AND FAMILY, MARKET LAVINGTON

BOWERCHALKE

## REAPERS AND GLEANERS

In the soft, warm summer-time, when the midsummer hum of the myriads of insects in the air sheds a drowsy harmony over the tree-tops, the field-faring woman goes out to hay-making, and leaves her baby in the shade by the hedge-side. A wooden sheepcage, turned upside down and filled with new-made hay, forms not at all a despicable cradle; and here the little thing lies on its back and inhales the fresh pure air, and feels the warmth of the genial sun, cheered from time to time by visits from its busy mother. Perhaps this is the only true poetry of the hayfield, so much talked of and praised. The mother works with her rake, or with a shorter, smaller prong; and if it is a large farm, the women are kept as much as possible together, for their strength and skill will not allow them to work at the same pace as the men, and if they work in company the one hinders the other. A man can do the work of two women, and do it better in every way, besides being capable of the heavier tasks of pitching, cock-making, &c., which the women cannot manage. Before the haymaking machines and horse-rakes came into vogue, it was not uncommon to see as many as twenty women following each other in *échelon*, turning a 'wallow,' or shaking up the green swathes left by the mowers. Farmers were obliged

to employ them, but were never satisfied with their work, which was the dearest they paid for. Somehow, there was no finish to it. Large numbers of women still work in the hayfield; but they are not used in gangs so much as formerly, but distributed about to do light jobs for which a man cannot be spared, and in these they are useful. The pay used to be tenpence a day; now it is one shilling and a pint of beer per day, and in some places fifteenpence. The Arcadian innocence of the hayfield, sung by the poets, is the most barefaced fiction; for those times are the rural saturnalia, and the broadest and coarsest of jokes and insinuations are freely circulated; nor does it always stop at language only, provided the master be out of sight. Matrons and young girls alike come in for an equal share of this rude treatment, and are quite a match for the men in the force of compliment. The women leave work an hour or so before the men, except when there is a press, and the farmer is anxious to get in the hay before a storm comes. It is not that the hayfield itself originates this coarseness, but this is almost the only time of the year when the labouring classes work together in large numbers. A great deal of farm-work is comparatively solitary; in harvest droves of people are collected together, and the inherent vulgarity comes out more strongly. At the wheat-harvest the women go reaping, and exceedingly hard they work at it.

BOWERCHALKE

There is no harder work done under the sun than reaping, if it is well followed up. From earliest dawn to latest night they swing the sickles, staying with their husbands, and brothers, and friends, till the moon silvers the yellow corn. The reason is because reaping is piece-work, and not paid by the day, so that the longer and the harder they work the more money is earned. In this a man's whole family can assist. His wife, his grown-up sons and daughters cut the corn, the younger ones can carry it and aid in various ways.

It is wonderful how the men stand the excessive and continuous labour; it is still more wonderful how the women endure it, trying as it is to the back. It is the hottest season of the year – the early autumn; the sun burns and scorches, and the warm wind gives no relief; even the evenings are close and sultry. The heated earth reflects the rays, and the straw is dry and warm to the touch. The standing corn, nearly as high as the reaper, keeps off the breeze, if there is any, from her brow. Grasping the straw continuously cuts and wounds the hand, and even gloves will hardly give perfect protection. The woman's bare neck is turned to the colour of tan; her thin muscular arms bronze right up to the shoulder. Short time is allowed for refreshment; right through the hottest part of the day they labour. It is remarkable that none, or very few, cases of sunstroke occur. Cases of vertigo and vomiting are frequent, but pass off in a few hours. Large quantities of liquor are taken to sustain the frame weakened by perspiration.

When night does arrive, even then the task is not over, for they have to carry home on their heads the bundle of wheat gleaned by the smaller children, and perhaps walk two miles to the cottage. This is indeed work for a woman still suckling her child. It is not easy to calculate what a woman earns at such seasons, because they rarely work on their own account: either the father or the husband receives the wages in a lump with his own; but it cannot be much less than that earned by a man; for at these times they work with a will, and they do not at the haymaking. While reaping the baby is nestled down on a heap of coats or shawls under the shelter of the shocks of corn, which form a little hut for it, and, as in the hayfield, is watched by one of the children. Often three or four women will place their babies close together, and leave one great girl in charge of the whole, which is an economy, releasing other children for work; for the hayfield and the corn-harvest are the labourer's gold-mine. There is not so much rough joking in the corn-field; they do not work so close together, and the husband or father is near at hand; neither is there time nor inclination in the midst of such severe labour, to which haymaking is play.

*Richard Jefferies*

TRUFFLE HUNTING, WINTERSLOW

## TRUFFLE HUNTERS AT WINTERSLOW

The Winter months used to be the peak season for trufflers, says a correspondent in yesterday's 'Times.' But who seeks truffles now? There is a fair demand for truffles imported in bottles and sold at prices which make them cost anywhere between 30s. and 60s. a pound, but there seems now to be not one man who makes a business of harvesting the subterranean fungus in England. Yet two generations ago truffle-hunting was a fairly well recognised occupation, and the village of Winterslow (sometimes described as the headquarters of English truffling) was said to contain at least 10 trufflers. Apparently Yeates was the family which produced the greatest number of active truffle-hunters, but the name of Collins may be even better known, since Mr. Eli Collins was the most famous truffle-finder of his time; indeed, his repute went beyond the borders of England.

*Salisbury Times, 23 December 1938*

THOMAS YEATES AND HIS TRUFFLE DOGS

RAMSBURY

WORTON SCHOOL

BISHOP'S CANNINGS

## RECTOR'S DAUGHTERS

At the end of the field, separated from it by a second ha-ha, stood the church.

It was a most beautiful building, of the Early English period, nobly proportioned and crowned with a graceful spire. Yet the intense love that we felt for it was not merely on account of its beauty, nor because we were particularly religious children, but rather because from our earliest days it was so closely bound up with our daily lives. Every time we looked out of the nursery window there it stood, like some friendly grey angel keeping watch over our little world. If we waked unhappy in the night we could peep through the panes and see it black against a screen of stars, or washed in silver in the moonlight – a perpetual symbol, to minds troubled by disordered dreams, of peace and safety. Often when we were returning from a long walk over the downs, a little tired and footsore perhaps, a sudden glimpse of that slender spire piercing the sky ahead would revive our sinking spirits: 'The church!' we would cry, and home would instantly seem very near at hand.

Or perhaps we might be playing in the garden and not quite know what to do with ourselves, the day being cold and dull and the earth empty of delights. Then someone would say, 'Let's go to the church!' and off we would trot, full of a new enthusiasm.

Passing through the little north door we entered into a vast and ancient world of enormous pillars towering up to the far-away roof, whence the carved heads of kings and bishops looked down at us with gravely staring eyes.

In the nave all was clearness and light, but beyond the central arch, shadows lay thick across the long chancel, and only the eastern window with its brilliant blue-and-red glass struck sharply through the twilight. Wandering in and out among the pillars we felt very small and yet immensely safe; no harm could ever come to us in the church. Even when once I had been sent after dark to find a bottle of sal-volatile in the vestry, because my father was ill, it was only while crossing the churchyard that I had known fear, and it had fled away so soon as I saw the pillars rising round me in the moonlight.

Sometimes, if the spirit moved us, we would climb into the pulpit and preach an imaginary sermon; there would be no words, but abundant gesture.

Sometimes we would sit beside the font and practise saying Amen in the deep, magnificent way in which the sexton, who was the village saddler, said it. Sometimes we scaled the narrow stairs to the priest's chamber above the vestry, and hunted hopefully among the litter for some relic of the past, or sometimes we went and sat quietly in the big box-like chair, or carrel, in the northern transept.

We were very proud of that chair, for we had been told that there was not another in England like it. On its high back panel was painted a huge hand, and on every finger and across the palm were inscribed little cheerless sentences about sin and death, such as, 'Thou knowest not how often, thou knowest not how much, thou hast

ALDBOURNE CARNIVAL

offended God', or, 'Thy end is bitter, thy life is short'. No one who had a guilty conscience at the moment cared to go and sit under that portentous hand, and even when entirely conscience-free, we did not linger too long within its range. We preferred to pass on and read aloud the inscription over the organ, which set forth that the native of the village who had given and endowed it for all time had sailed round the world with our hero, Captain Cook. That was another matter for pride; we did not suppose that any other village in England had an organ bequeathed by a man who had sailed with Captain Cook.

But all attractions that the church could offer grew pale beside the fascination of the belfry and the tower. No sooner did we feel the first step of the spiral staircase beneath our feet than our hearts began to beat faster, and of all the hundreds of times we must have climbed it, never do I once remember the sense of adventure to have failed.

The belfry was quickly reached. It was a circular room with many windows and a deep stone recess to each. Here were usually to be found little heaps of hazel-shells left by the ringers, who seemed to have a squirrel-like capacity for nuts, and sometimes careful search would reveal an uncracked one among the rest. Often, too, there were a few empty beer-bottles.

Mr father never tried to prevent the ringers from thus refreshing themselves, but when he quitted the parish an

ascetic and fussy curate was left in charge for a time, and he soon put a stop to the beer and the nuts. But he also managed by general tactlessness to put a stop to the good will of the ringers, who gave up their job in a body and never returned to it again, although some of them had rung the bells regularly for twenty or thirty years.

Through the ceiling of the belfry long ropes slid mysteriously down and ended in brightly striped woollen handles, soft and pleasant to hold.

We ourselves were taught to chime at a very early age, so that we might supply the place of the ringers at week-day services, and as we grew older and stronger we were gradually promoted to the far more exciting, albeit dangerous, art of ringing. What a bracing but terrifying thought it was that if you mishandled your bell he might in revenge carry you up to the ceiling – even, may be, with such force that the ceiling would give way and you would be carried clean through it to the home of the bells.

In the belfry was a door that opened on to the outer roof of the nave, whose smooth grey leads provided just the right surface for tobogganing. Unfettered by any misgivings as to the effect on our clothes, we would slide down time after time, running up the steep slope again without a thought of fear. Our parents, to the surprise of many neighbours, never raised any objection to this pastime, either on the score of irreverence or of danger. My father was too genuinely religious a man to look for irreverence where he knew none existed, and my mother wise enough

PEA-PICKERS, LITTLE CHEVERELL.

to feel that a child's greatest safety lies in the absence of fear.

My father himself, though he never joined us in our sliding, liked to stand on the roof and cool himself after some strenuous ringing. One winter night he had remained behind the ringers to tidy up the belfry, and afterwards he stepped out through the door and stayed there a little while enjoying the cool frosty air and the brilliant stars. Suddenly a gust of wind slammed the door behind him, and since there was no handle on the outside of it, there he was, shut out on the roof of the church with never a soul to set him free.

*Ida Gandy*

## THE LITTLE STEEPLE

There is another feature of the church which must be mentioned now because up to some fifty years ago it played an important part in the traditional character of Cannings. This is the squat little steeple that nestles against the NE side of the spire. A long time ago, the inhabitants won a reputation for being exceptionally simple, and the most widely current of all the stories illustrating their simplicity relates to this little steeple. Its apparent absurdity provided the people in surrounding villages and in

BISHOP'S CANNINGS CHURCH

ALDBOURNE BAND

Devizes with an excellent excuse for teasing, since they saw it as something as childish and immature as those who lived beneath it. Driven by shame and exasperation, the inhabitants are reported to have carried up a load of manure and planted it round the stones. Then, when the grass began to grow freely they dragged a calf up the steep spiral staircase to eat it down. And in the latter part of the nineteenth century it was still the fashion at Devizes market to greet a Cannings man with derisive laughter and such questions as, 'Hast dunged thy little steeple yet?' or 'Beant it time to dung 'un again?'

In my own childhood the roadman would forestall any jokes at his expense when a traveller stopped to ask the name of the village by replying, 'That's Bishops Cannings – where us dunged the little steeple.'

Yet in spite of all the gibes that small steeple is no odd irrelevant addition. It looked down on the world some 200 years before the spire, and serves its own proper purpose of providing an exit from the spiral staircase. Therefore it should be treated with the respect that it deserves. Just as the true native of Bishops Cannings is shrewder than he first appears so there is more to the little steeple than strikes the casual observer.

*Ida Gandy*

## IN CHITTERNE CHURCHYARD

Chitterne is one of those small out-of-the world villages in the south Wiltshire downs which attract one mainly because of their isolation and loneliness and their unchangeableness. Here, however, you discover that there has been an important change in comparatively recent years – some time during the first half of the last century. Chitterne, like most villages, possesses one church, a big building with a tall spire standing in its central part. Before it was built there were two churches and two Chitternes – two parishes with one village, each with its own proper church. These were situated at opposite ends of the one long street, and were small ancient buildings, each standing in its own churchyard. One of these disused burying-places, with a part of the old building still standing in it, is a peculiarly attractive spot, all the more so because of a long years of neglect and of ivy, bramble, and weed and flower of many kinds that flourish in it, and have long obliterated the mounds and grown over the few tombs and headstones that still exist in the ground.

It was an excessively hot August afternoon when I last visited Chitterne, and, wishing to rest for an hour before proceeding on my way, I went to this old churchyard, naturally thinking that I should have it all to myself. But I found two persons there, both old women of the peasant

CHITTERNE

class, meanly dressed; yet it was evident they had their good clothes on and were neat and clean, each with a basket on her arm, probably containing her luncheon. For they were only visitors and strangers there, and strangers to one another as they were to me – that, too, I could guess: also that they had come there with some object – perhaps to find some long unvisited grave, for they were walking about, crossing and recrossing each other's track, pausing from time to time to look round, then pulling the ivy aside from some old tomb and reading or trying to read the worn, moss-grown inscription. I began to watch their movements with growing interest, and could see that they, too, were very much interested in each other, although for a long time they did not exchange a word. Presently I, too, fell to examining the gravestones, just to get near them, and while pretending to be absorbed in the inscriptions I kept a sharp eye on their movements. They took no notice of me. I was nothing to them – merely one of another class, a foreigner, so to speak, a person cycling about the country who was just taking a ten minutes' peep at the place to gratify an idle curiosity. But who was *she* – that other old woman; and what did she want hunting about there in this old forsaken churchyard? was doubtless what each of those two was saying to herself. And by-and-by their curiosity got the better of them; they contrived to meet at one stone which they both appeared anxious to examine.

I had anticipated this, and no sooner were they together

than I was down on my knees busily pulling the ivy aside from a stone three or four yards from theirs, absorbed in my business. They bade each other good day and said something about the hot weather, which led one on to remark that she had found it very trying as she had left home early to walk to Salisbury to take the train to Codford, and from there she had walked again to Chitterne. Oddly enough, the other old woman had also been travelling all day, but from an opposite direction, over Somerset way, just to visit Chitterne. It seemed an astonishing thing to them when it came out that they had both been looking forward for years to this visit, and that it should have been made on the same day, and that they should have met there in that same forsaken little graveyard. It seemed stranger still when they came to tell why they had made this long-desired visit. They were both natives of the village, and had both left it early in life, one aged seven, the other ten; they had left much about the same time, and had never returned until now. And they were now here with the same object – just to find the graves, unmarked by a stone, where the mother of one of them, the grandparents of both, and other relatives they still remembered had been buried more than half a century ago. They were surprised and troubled at their failure to identify the very spots where the mounds used to be. 'It do all look so different,' said one, 'an' the old stones be mostly gone.' Finally, when they told their names and their fathers' names – farm-labourers both – they failed to

SEEND CHURCH

remember each other, and could only suppose that they must have forgotten many things about their far-off childhood, although others were still as well remembered as the incidents of yesterday.

The old dames had become very friendly and confidential by this time. 'I dare say,' I said to myself, 'that if I can manage to stay to the end I shall see them embrace and kiss at parting,' and I also thought that their strange meeting in the old village churchyard would be a treasured memory for the rest of their lives. I feared they would suspect me of eavesdropping, and taking out my penknife, I began diligently scraping the dead black moss from the letters on the stone, after which I made pretence of copying the illegible inscription in my notebook. They, however, took no notice of me, and began telling each other what their lives had been since they left Chitterne. Both had married working men and had lost their husbands many years ago; one was sixty-nine, the other in her sixty-sixth year, and both were strong and well able to work, although they had had hard lives. Then, in a tone of triumph, their faces lighting up with a kind of joy, they informed each other that they had never had to go to the parish for relief. Each was anxious to be first in telling how it had come about that she, the poor widow of a working man, had been so much happier in her old age than so many others. So eager were they to tell it that when one

spoke the other would cut in long before she finished, and when they talked together it was not easy to keep the two narratives distinct. One was the mother of four daughters, all still unmarried, earning their own livings, one in a shop, another a sempstress, two in service in good houses, earning good wages. Never had woman been so blessed in her children! They would never see their mother go to the House! The other had but one, a son, and not many like him; no son ever thought more of his mother. He was at sea, but every nine to ten months he was back in Bristol, and then on to visit her, and never let a month pass without writing to her and sending money to pay her rent and keep a nice comfortable home for him.

They congratulated one another; then the mother of four said she always thanked God for giving her daughters, because they were women and could feel for a mother. The other replied that it was true, she had often seen it, the way daughters stuck to their mother – until they married. She was thankful to have a son; a man, she said, is a man and can go out in the world and do things, and if he is a good son he will never see his mother want.

The other was nettled at that speech. 'Of course a man's a man,' she returned, 'but we all know what men are. They are all right till they pick up with a girl who wants all their wages; then everyone, mother and all, must be given up.' But a daughter was a daughter always; she had four,

SAIL REAPER

she was happy to say.

This made matters worse. 'Daughters always daughters!' came the quick rejoinder. 'I never learned that before. What, my son take up with a girl and leave his old mother to starve or go to the workhouse! I never heard such a foolish thing said in my life!' And, being now quite angry, she looked round for her basket and shawl so as to get away as quickly as possible from that insulting woman; but the other, guessing her intention, was too quick for her and started at once to the gate, but after going four or five steps turned and delivered her last shot: 'Say what you like about your son, and I don't doubt he's been good to you, and I only hope it'll always be the same; but what I say is, give me a daughter, and I know, ma'am, that if you had a daughter you'd be easier in your mind!'

Having spoken, she made for the gate, and the other, stung in some vital part by the last words, stood motionless, white with anger, staring after her, first in silence, but presently she began talking audibly to herself. 'My son – my son pick up with a girl! My son leave his mother to go on the parish!' – but I stayed to hear no more; it made me laugh and – it was too sad.

*W.H. Hudson*

## REAPERS

The reapers were at work in the wheat, but the plain was so level that it was not possible to see them without mounting upon a flint heap. Then their heads were just visible as they stood upright, but when they stooped to use the hook they disappeared. Yonder, however, a solitary man in his shirt-sleeves perched up above the corn went round and round the field, and beside him strange awkward arms seemed to beat down the wheat. He was driving a reaping machine, to which the windmill-like arms belonged. Beside the road a shepherd lingered, leaning on a gate, while his flock, which he was driving just as fast and no faster than they cared to eat their way along the sward, fed part on one side and part on the other. Now and then two or three sheep crossed over with the tinkling of a bell. In the silence and stillness and brooding heat, the larks came and dusted themselves in the white impalpable powder of the road. Farther away the partridges stole quietly to an anthill at the edge of some barley. By the white road, a while milestone, chipped and defaced, stood almost hidden among thistles and brambles. Some white railings guarded the sides of a bridge, or rather a low arch over a dry watercourse. Heat, dust, a glaring whiteness, and a boundless expanse of golden wheat on either hand.

*Richard Jefferies*

## THRESHING

Our threshing machine was driven by a seven horse-power portable steam-engine, which was in the capable hands of one, Thomas Toomer. He ran the engine, and Charlie Bailey, the mower referred to at the beginning of this book, fed the sheaves into the threshing machine.

On threshing days they would leave home much earlier than the other men, to get steam up and everything in readiness for a seven o'clock start in the morning. For this

WINTERBOURNE MONCKTON

extra work and for covering up the tackle with tarpaulins at night, they received one shilling per day extra.

They were not supposed to light the fire in the engine if it looked like rain, and rarely was their judgment at fault.

There was a balanced team of men to run the outfit. Two men pitched the sheaves on to the top of the thresher, where one man cut the strings and another fed the grain steadily and smoothly into the machine. Two men made the straw rick, one took off the chaff, and one the grain, whilst Tom, the driver, was in charge of the machinery. Any one man slackening speed would slow up the whole business. No extra money was paid to the regular farm men for threshing, but beer was allowed on threshing days, one quart per man. Personally I did not like threshing as the dust made me sneeze continuously all day, but I have done every job in connection with it, even to minding the chaff or dust, as it was termed locally. That was a dirty job. You stood in a narrow passage-way between the machine and the corn rick, and worked in a dust cloud all day. The man who usually did it had whiskers growing out of his nose, and these would be festooned with cobwebs in the first hour.

Tom and Charlie must have known much more about machinery than I gave them credit for in my unthinking youth, as I cannot ever remember a serious breakdown,

and their reliability was extraordinary. On the evening before a threshing day you just said: 'Oh, Tom, we shall be 'sheening' to-morrow,' and, if fine, when you arrived at the ricks at 7 a.m. on a January morning, say, you would find Tom standing in the glow of the fire with wisps of steam playing around his head. And the old boy had left his home at 5 a.m., and walked perhaps a mile and a half to the ricks!

'Now then, chaps. Let's 'ave you,' the foreman would say. Some men would strip the thatch from the rick, whilst others would pile it out of the way of the machinery. Charlie would mount to his feeder's place on top of the thresher, and his mate would sharpen his knife on a whetstone. When all was ready, Tom would shout: 'All right?' 'Ay, Tom. Let her goo.' Tom would push the throttle lever a little, the driving belt would tighten, clap once or twice, and in a moment or two the rich hum of the thresher would fill the countryside, and dominate all of us till lunch time at nine-thirty.

Ricks which were not threshed until after Christmas usually contained some rats, and this added a spice of sport to the finish of the day's work, as most of them remained hidden until the bottom layer of sheaves was moved. They were killed ruthlessly; a pitchfork is an efficient weapon for this purpose.

AVEBURY

At some time in the forenoon Tommy and the trap would arrive bringing the master mind. My father would inspect the corn by dipping his hand into a full sack, a method of judging whether the corn was dry; you cannot push your hand into a damp sack of wheat. A handful would then be smelled vigorously. I can see them at it now, with grains of corn adhering to my father's moustache and the foreman's whiskers. Before he left father would study the portion of the corn rick still unthreshed, with a shrewd, calculating eye, and say to the forman: 'Well, you'll be able to finish all right in nice time?'

*A.G. Street*

## A YOUTHFUL BURGLAR

At the Town Hall, yesterday before H. Moulton, esq., *Albert Henry Humphries*, aged 12½ years, son of Job Humphries, cloth worker, was charged with burglariously breaking into a cottage occupied by Lydia Chesterman, at Bearfield, during the night of Sunday last, and stealing 1s. in money, also a piece of pudding and a piece of cake – A niece who was sleeping in the house heard a noise downstairs about 2 a.m., but feared to awake the other inmates, and in the morning it was discovered that a pane of glass had been removed from the kitchen window and the fastening lifted, by which means entrance was effected, and the little urchin also left by the same means, but left behind a females woollen vest, which led to his arrest. – The several witnesses were examined, when the magistrate remanded the prisoner until to-day, when he will probably be birched.

*Devizes and Wiltshire Gazette, 4 April 1889*

## ELI MATTHEWS

Until his retirement he was a woodman on Priory Farm. Some forty years ago he used to offend his congregation's sense of propriety by preaching in his smock. Yet, being fond of him and unwilling to hurt his feelings, they did not know how to bring to his notice the unseemliness of his costume. At length they thought of a tactful solution, and made some anniversary the excuse for presenting him with a best suit. What was their dismay to see him arrive at chapel on the following Sunday wearing the smock over

STONEHENGE ENCLOSURE PROTEST

his suit, lest its smartness should be impaired.

Had the villagers but known it, the smock was infinitely superior to the suit. It was a garment reversible from back to front, and was made of unbleached handspun linen, smocked with white linen thread at the chest, back, wrists and shoulders, and feather-stitched at collar, cuffs and 'boxes' – the flat panels on either side of the front and back smocking – with formal designs of trees and leaves symbolical of the woodman's craft. (For the embroidery of a smock varied according to the occupation of the wearer. A shepherd's might be recognised by its curly crooks, a gardener's by its flowers, a dairymaid's by its pattern of hearts.) To be sure, it fitted the figure even less than the ready-made suit; but, then, it made no pretence of doing so. It was designed to be worn over coats on cold days or instead of them in summer, and so to turn up or down at the collar, while the nature of the stitchery provided a certain amount of elasticity and incidentally gave extra warmth in the most necessary places. Eli's smock must have been one of the last of its kind.

*Heather and Robin Tanner*

## STONEHENGE

*To the Editor of the Devizes and Wiltshire Gazette.*
Sir, – In accordance with the advice given to me by various bodies interested in antiquarian and archaeological research. I have given orders that Stonehenge shall be enclosed on the 24th inst.

It is my intention, however, but without relinquishing any of my rights as owner of the property, to admit visitors within the enclosure on payment of 1s. each person, on the understanding that they will conform to the authority of the custodian and the regulations laid down for their guidance.

May I take this opportunity of requesting all visitors to assist the custodian in enforcing the regulations which have been framed with the object of preventing injury to the stones by thoughtless persons and for the general preservation of this unique monument.

I am, Sir, your obedient servant,
E. ANTROBUS.
Amesbury Abbey, 16th May, 1901.

SALISBURY FAIR

## FAIR

When the fair came for three days in October, it completely dominated us. If someone had said, 'This is what heaven will be like. Up there, all this goes on the whole time', we should haver felt quite ready to die at once. But our role was very much that of spectators. No grown-up who took us to the fair ever wanted to go on anything. If Nanny had been put on a horse, or plumped inside a dragon on the switch-back, she would probably have died – not from a desire to go to an everlasting fair but from dizzy, terrified abhorrence. When we were small, Helen and I went on the children's roundabout. This was rotated by a boy who stood in the middle turning a handle. The day we went on a cock and a hen, his nose was bleeding. He didn't wipe it. He let it bleed. . . . We never went on the big roundabouts. Helen, who was prone to sickness when she travelled, did not want to travel on a grown-up horse. I was too frightened. And neither of us would have been allowed to embark on such peril by Nanny had we wanted to. Much of the fun was to

stare goggle-eyed at those who were being torn round at such a horrifying speed, and to snuggle our toes deeper into our boots with a splendid sense of personal deliverance, strongly fostered by Nanny. But occasionally, at the sight of a child whizzing nonchalantly round, or simply to indulge in heroic drama, one would moot the question: 'S'pose I went on it, Nanny?'

'You wouldn't like it – you'd be sick.'

'But s'pose I did?' Nanny's certainty that it was quite out of the question and would be sheer disaster, helped to stifle one's discomfort at seeing a contemporary apparently enjoying that terrifying ordeal.

But Ena and Sylvia did go on the big roundabout. We watched them going round and round – whirl – whirl . . . Ena waved, but Sylvia was quite bent up. . . .

We were never taken into the side-shows. The Fat Woman fed on pork pies was considered vulgar, and to go and stare at her was not at all a nice way of spending sixpence. And it was not kind to go and gape at the Human Monster with Lobster Claws. She had been born like that, and to go and deliberately stare at her in a tent

WILLIAM TAYLOR'S SIDESHOW

was even worse than staring at a deformity in the street. The dancer who divested herself of seven veils shouldn't do such a thing. Anyone should be ashamed to be seen looking at her. Nanny said we didn't want to stand and watch the two girls in black lace stockings and pink satin bloomers with spangles on them, either – but Sylvia did. 'No you don't,' said Nanny. 'You want to see the gold-fish.'

*Geraldine Symons*

## FAIR DAYS

On fair days the men drove the sale sheep to the fair in the early morning, and were then finished for the day. This fair was a business one in the morning, and a pleasure fair in the evening. In addition to sheep selling it was the recognized hiring fair. Men in search of a new situation wore the badge of their calling in their hats. A carter wore a plait of whipcord, a shepherd a tuft of wool, and cowmen sported some hair from a cow's tail.

Men were hired from Michaelmas, October 11th, for the year, usually by verbal agreement, the essential features of this being noted down in the farmer's pocket-book. All sorts of things came under review during the discussion of these agreements. You might agree with a man subject to a favourable character from his present employer, to find on inquiry that although he was all right, his wife was of a quarrelsome disposition. This might be a hopeless drawback. A farmer doesn't just employ a man, and remain in ignorance of his life during non-working hours. He has to live with him, and these domestic differences can upset the whole farm.

The pleasure fair in the evening was a whirl of round-abouts, swinging boats, coconut shies, shooting galleries and sideshows and cheapjacks of all kinds, the whole place being lit up in the evening with reeking naphtha flares. Here rural youth made high holiday.

In my childhood days, I can remember being lifted on to a bench, and, kneeling there, shooting with an airgun at a bull's eye on a large box some two yards away. When you hit the mark, the lid of the box flew open, and a large

THE RINK, SWINDON

stuffed monkey on a piece of elastic jumped out.

Then there was the 'Bombardment of Alexandria' in a large tent. This was a glorified magic lantern show, the forerunner of moving pictures. I have never enjoyed any London theatre more than I did that crude entertainment in my boyhood.

There were 'Try your strength' towers, where you drove a weight with a large mallet up the tower where it rang a bell if you got it to the top. Farmers and labourers vied with each other at this trial of strength. One of our men could do this one-handed with ease, and used to coach the inefficient, much as a golf professional in later years supervised my beginner's efforts. The words used by each teacher are different, but the meaning is the same. 'Doan't 'ee goo at un zo ravish. You wants to take it easy and suent, zno, but you wants to ketch un jist right. Like this.'

*A.G. Street*

## THE MARLBOROUGH MOP

The annual statute hiring fair at Marlborough was held, as is usual, in the High Street. But a pleasure fair on a more

elaborate footing followed on Saturday last. The wide and historical street, the pride of Marlborough, was besieged with the accustomed paraphernalia of a pleasure fair. There was an unmistakeable cheerfulness in the disposition of everybody, and a scene of hilarity which is only revived once a year. The hiring fair is a day when the farmer and his servant meet to make fresh bargains in the way of engagements. The subsequent fair is a time of rejoicing, and so on Saturday the tillers of the soil for miles around flocked into the town and made their way to the Mop – for such is the title of the fair. All along the High Street were stalls, shows, shooting galleries and a complement of other attractions, in fact, the whole town may be said to have been in the hands of showmen. There is a contentedness about these people which one cannot fail to detect. Their caravans serve as their place of abode, but they prefer the open air for the consumption of their diet. Their cooking is done by means of camp fires, and Saturday morning saw several of these in various parts of the streets, with pans and other kitchen utensils serving their purpose. At dinner hour temporary dining tables made out of boxes and planks were rigged up in the steet, and the show-people consumed their victuals with no concern for the curious attention they received from the pedestrians. As

MARLBOROUGH MOP FAIR

evening set in the 'fun of the fair' commenced in earnest. The street was brilliantly illuminated by numerous small electric lights and it wore a picturesque and animated appearance. Throngs of busy and bustling people; the din of half-a-dozen organs airing different tunes; stentorian voices of the showmen endeavouring to convince the community that under their respective canvas the best value for money was obtained. At one establishment, a roaring trade was done, the crowds being enticed by the performances of four 'damsels' attired in glittering panto-mimic costumes, on a stage outside. At another a crowd who were hesitating at the doors were told in all earn-estness that it was well to 'enjoy yourselves while you live, for you'll be a long time dead.' The unsophisticated maiden found rare sport in the confetti bag and their lovers and would-be lovers received more than their due atten-tion. The younger fraternity were well catered for, the switchback and the round-about proving the great attrac-tion. The fair on the whole was considered an average one but there were many new and novel features. Among them were several exhibitions of animated photographs, including one at which was to be seen a reproduction of the scene witnessed in the Marlborough Market Place at midday on Saturday.

*Marlborough Times, 19 October 1901*

THE TAYLOR DANCING GIRLS

YOUNG PLOUGHMAN, AVEBURY

## EARLY MORNING

The pale beams of the waning moon still cast a shadow on the cottage, when the labourer rises from his heavy sleep on a winter's morning. Often he huddles on his things and slips his feet into his thick 'water-tights' – which are stiff and hard, having been wet over night – by no other light than this. If the household is comparatively well managed, however, he strikes a match, and his 'dip' shows at the window. But he generally prefers to save a candle, and clatters down the narrow steep stairs in the semi-darkness, takes a piece of bread and cheese, and steps forth into the sharp air. The cabbages in the garden he notes are covered with white frost, so is the grass in the fields, and the footpath is hard under foot. In the furrows is a little ice – white because the water has shrunk from beneath it, leaving it hollow – and on the stile is a crust of rime, cold to the touch, which he brushes off in getting over. Overhead the sky is clear – cloudless but pale – and the stars, though not yet fading, have lost the brilliant glitter of midnight. Then, in all their glory, the idea of their globular shape is easily accepted; but in the morning, just as the dawn is breaking, the absence of glitter conveys the impression of flatness — circular rather than globular. But yonder, over the elms, above the cowpens, the great morning star has risen, shining far brighter, in proportion, than the moon; an intensely clear metallic light – like incandescent silver.

The shadows of the trees on the frosted ground are dull.

HEYTESBURY

DROVE ROAD, SWINDON

As the footpath winds by the hedge the noise of his footstep startles the blackbird roosting in the bushes, and he bustles out and flies across the field. There is more rime on the posts and rails around the rickyard, and the thatch on the haystack is white with it in places. He draws out the broad hay-knife – a vast blade, wide at the handle, the edge gradually curving to a point – and then searches for the rubber or whet-stone, stuck somewhere in the side of the rick. At the first sound of the stone upon the steel the cattle in the adjoining yard and sheds utter a few low 'moos,' and there is a stir among them. Mounting the ladder he forces the knife with both hands into the hay, making a square cut which bends outwards, opening from the main mass till it appears on the point of parting and letting him fall with it to the ground. But long practice has taught him how to balance himself half on the ladder, half on the hay. Presently, with a truss unbound and loose on his head, he enters the yard, and passes from crib to crib, leaving a little here and a little there. For if he fills one first, there will be quarrelling among the cows, and besides, if the crib is too liberally filled, they will pull it out and tread it under foot. The cattle that are in the sheds fattening for Christmas have cake as well, and this must be supplied in just proportion.

The hour of milking, which used to be pretty general everywhere, varies now in different places, to suit the necessities of the milk trade. The milk has, perhaps, to travel three or four miles to the railway station; near great towns, where some of the farmers deliver milk themselves from house to house, the cows are milked soon after noonday. What would their grandfathers have said to that? But where the old customs have not much altered, the milker sits down in the morning to his cow with the stars still visible overhead, punching his hat well into her side – a hat well battered and thickly coated with grease, for the skin of the cow exudes an unctuous substance. This hat he keeps for the purpose. A couple of milking pails – they are of large size – form a heavy load when filled. The milker, as he walks back to the farmhouse, bends his head under the yoke – whence so many men are round-shouldered – and steps slowly with a peculiar swaying motion of the body, which slight swing prevents it from spilling.

Another man who has to be up while the moon casts a shadow is the carter, who must begin to feed his team very early in order to get them to eat sufficient. If the manger be over-filled they spill and waste it, and at the same time will not eat so much. This is tedious work. Then the lads come and polish up the harness, and so soon as it is well light get out to plough. The custom with the horses is to begin to work as early as possible, but to strike off in the afternoon some time before the other men, the lads riding home astride. The strength of the carthorse has to be husbanded

THE SMITHY, FIGHELDEAN

carefully, and the labour performed must be adjusted to it and to the food – *i.e.*, fuel, consumed. To manage a large team of horses, so as to keep them in good condition, with glossy coats and willing step, and yet to get the maximum of work out of them, requires long experience and constant attention. The carter, therefore, is a man of much importance on a farm.

*Richard Jefferies*

## SALISBURY

Escape of a Prisoner. – A man named Harry Warren, who was in custody at the County Police Station on a charge of stealing watches at Downton, effected his escape on Wednesday, and has not been re-captured. Warren was seen in his cell by the constable on duty just before five o'clock in the afternoon. The constable was called to another part of the station, and when he returned to the cells some ten minutes later, he found that Warren's cell door was open and that the prisoner was gone. Inquiries were at once set on foot, and it was ascertained that Warren had been seen to leave the station premises by the yard gates. The cell doors at this station are of open work bars; and the keys were hung on a hook opposite the doors, but separated by the width of the passage. Warren had several papers in his cell, and these he rolled up and

tied together with boot-laces, being enabled in this fashion to reach the keys and bring them within reach of his hand. News of the prisoner's escape was at once communicated to the police, and inquiries made far and wide.

*Marlborough Times, 2 November 1901*

## THE FORGE

In the centre of the smithy is the forge, with its flat hearth on one side of the huge brick chimney and its leathern bellows on the other. A small red fire glows on the hearth. From time to time Henry replenishes it with a shovelful of slack. The shovel is hand made, as are all his tools. They show his resource and ingenuity – his recognition of the end desired and the most economical and efficient means of achieving it. Here is a small wide borax spoon; the end of its long handle curls into a hook by which it can hang, and towards the head it is twisted, for this is one of those good old tools that serve a double purpose – the spiral part of the handle is used as a file. In the trough of water at the end of the hearth is a 'swop,' a small bundle of rushes fixed in an iron handle. This is dabbed on to the heated iron when it requires cooling; it also comes in handy for scattering the crowd of small boys whose curiosity draws them within the half-door and too near the forge. On its massive wooden block stands the anvil, its beak pointed towards the hearth. Close by are ranged other things that

CALNE

must lie ready to hand: the tripod on which the horse rests its hoof while being shod; hammers, chisels, nails, punches, drills, tongs and pincers of various shapes and sizes, and an implement so necessary that it is called simply 'the tool,' or sometimes, because it is a good substitute for a second pair of hands, 'the boy.' This is a rough iron gauge that can hold the tongs in three different positions. Another improvisation is the 'axo' (hack-saw), a piece of an old scythe with one edge toothed so that it can be used for cutting iron. Occasionally, especially if it be winter, darkness falls before work is done, and light is needed. So the smith makes himself candlesticks of the material available. The candle needs a sconce; it must have a stem long enough to throw the light down; so thus it is made. The stem has to be set in a firm, well-weighted base. What could be better than a good heavy horse-shoe, with nail-holes already made for sockets? Or there is an old rushlight holder, that only needs a candle sconce to make it once more a useful means of illumination.

*Heather and Robin Tanner*

## PAY DAY

What a business it was! The yellow canvas bag had a partition dividing the gold from the silver, for we had gold in those days. Most farmers paid fortnightly, but my father always said that the money was of more value to the men if they got it weekly, and paid accordingly. He made a special point of going round the farm and paying the men at their work. There were no time-sheets. 'What do you make it this week, Tom?' my father would ask one of the labourers. 'Two and a half days fer you, zur, four hours overtime, and t'other hoeing.' 'What'll you draw on the hoeing?' The hoeing was piecework, and the 'two and a half days fer you' day work. 'Aight shillin', zur, and I've a ketched two dozen moles.' And from his pocket Tom would produce a grimy screw of paper containing twenty-four moles' tails, for which he would be paid one penny each.

*A.G. Street*

SPOTTED COW INN, COATE

## SHOOTING POACHERS

The sport of shooting poachers, which comes in towards Christmas, is now in full swing, some capital sport has already been obtained, and there appears to be a plentiful supply of human game on hand. Bands of men go into the woods armed with guns, and bands of men carrying revolvers go to meet them. The savage encounters that ensue read like those with banditti in the days of Königsmark the Robber. Indeed, while our expedition toils up the Nile (to rescue Gordon) and correspondents have little to describe beyond hard rowing, another war is proceeding at home, accompanied with serious bloodshed. If a 'special' were on the spot he would have to relate something like this. The keepers on a large preserve, by means of scouts and vedettes, ascertain the probable intentions of a gang of poachers, and settle themselves in ambush as the night approaches. They are well armed with breech-loading guns and revolvers, six-shooters, in American 'frontier' style, as if for a battle with Indians. The poachers, not having wealthy people to buy good weapons for them, generally have old muzzle-loading guns, and have not yet arrived at the civilization of the revolver. Heavy shadows settle in the hollow by the firs; it is night, and by-and-by a scout creeps up with the intelligence that the enemy is busy at the side of the plantation. Fetching a detour the 'frontier' men suddenly rush out from a gateway. There is a scuffle – curses – quick flashes of red flame light up the scene. On one side a curl of white smoke ascends from the barrel of a levelled gun. On the other a curl of smoke darts from a revolver extended by an arm in velveteen. Two more men are rolling over each other on the ground, bound up inextricably in a great net into which they have fallen and drawn round them. Another lies twisted in a heap, doubled up, hard hit; a pheasant projects from his coat-pocket. Bang! bang! There are groans, curses, a lantern is turned on, and the fight is over. Next morning, if you visited the spot early, you might see scene two. On the wet grass, stained cartridge-cases; marks of heavy iron-shod boots dug deeply into the soil in the struggle; a broken pipe; a hare wire; blood on the grass and on the crushed bunch of rushes, blood which remains though a fine rain is falling, and drip, dripping from the still trees. Some pheasant feathers lie scattered by the ditch. Away in a shed a stiff and human carcass is extended under a sheet. Other human game, wounded but not mortally, is bagged in the cells at the nearest town. Cold and wet the grey winter's morning casts its chill over the view: this is the time to think of the fatherless children and the widow. Is not this a noble sport for Christmas-

NORTH STREET, WILTON

tide? A grand subject here for the next Academy Exhibition, two panels – (I) 'The Battle': (2) 'Next Morning'.

'The right to kill!' A fresh addition to the rights of man, invented when Madame Clovis Hugues shot M. Morin. In Paris you may avenge your honour – at least, a lady may; these are privileged cases. In England – moral England, which expressed such horror – everybody has a right to kill – a poacher. A keeper is a licensed killer; he shoots cats, weasels, crows, poachers, and other vermin equally. It is his royal pleasure – the keeper *s'amuse*. The boost of our civilization is the high value we set upon human life. Never, never before in the whole history of man was life so sacred as it is now. The tribunals hold that even starvation does not justify homicide. What, then, can justify this shooting of poachers? Of course a poacher is engaged in an unlawful act, but is that act sufficiently unlawful to render it right to kill him? He is not a burglar, he does not enter a house and put the lives of the inmates in danger. He is not a garrotter – he does not attack people with violence in the street. A wood is not a house – nor even a garden. The argument that he goes by night is merely a legal quibble – poaching by night is the same in this respect as poaching by day; neither by day nor night is there any assault. The poacher, in short, is simply a thief who steals rabbits and pheasants instead of watches from a shop window. It is not nearly so much an assault upon the person as stealing without violence, from the pocket. A man has his pocket picked at Charing-Cross Station; Policeman B. witnesses the robbery, runs up and seizes the thief; suppose Policeman B. drew a revolver from his breast and shot the thief instead? Would that be justifiable? It even remains a moot point what does and what does not

BISHOPSTONE

MANOR COTTAGES, AVEBURY

justify one in shooting a burglar. Only a poacher may be shot with impunity.

But a poacher goes armed, true, but with the purpose of shooting pheasants. The keeper does not shoot pheasants at night, nor at any time, with revolvers; such weapons are intended to be used upon man. Those who have had any experience of the combative instincts of rude men know very well that there are many keepers – and others – who go to these brutal encounters with delight. Cases have been seen even of young farmers joining the keeper's gang to enjoy the battle. It is altogether nonsense to suppose that they go out armed with revolvers with the purely virtuous intention of protecting property. They like the row; they like to 'do' for somebody. Good keepers are perfectly well acquainted with various ways and means of tracking and identifying poachers, and if the present be not sufficient some one should invent a portable electric lantern to be suddenly turned on, and so, by making the covers as light as day, afford a view. Poachers would dread a bright light – which means identification – far more than gunpowder. The truth is that these bloodthirsty affairs are a disgrace to our boasted humanity. We have just had an outburst of indignation against keepers shooting cats; but

shooting a poacher is nothing – it does not happen in Bulgaria, and is no atrocity. The truth also is that these bloodthirsty businesses are part and parcel of a marked change of tone in the population, they belong to the same class of sentiment that promotes prize-fighting, now so much on the increase. It is downright brutality, and nothing else. It is most injurious to the interest of sport, against which it must ultimately create a prejudice.

*Richard Jefferies*

## OLD RICKS

Uncle Dicky always had a vast number of corn-ricks about the farm; he was never in a hurry to thresh out. Sometimes a stack stood a dozen years before being cleared of the grain – that is, what the rats and mice had not been able to devour in the time. People said he was a miser and did not want the money, but that was not true. If he had been a miser he would have threshed the ricks and made sure of it, and hoarded the gold. I have heard of a wheatstack that stood for thirty-two years, though there could not poss-

GYPSY FAMILY, WARMINSTER

ibly have been anything left but straw and 'chammings.' When Farmer Westell threshed a rick of beans last year, that had only stood two summers, the men killed no less than one hundred and forty-eight rats, and several hundred mice. This was a great day for the hens in the farmyard; they waited around the threshing tackle and caught the rodents as they ran off, and devoured them with great satisfaction; they are very fond of mice.

*Alfred Williams*

## PLAIN FOOD

The villagers' food, especially that of the labouring class, is plain and simple in kind, but plentiful enough. The chief article consumed is bread, and abundant potatoes; where there is a large family of six or eight, the household requires eight or nine gallons of bread a week, or more, and then the wife and mother cooks potatoes for dinner and tea as well. The chief trimmings are Canadian bacon and cheese, butter or margarine, lard or dripping. The children eat bread and lard, with pepper upon it. When I

was a child, my mother used to buy dripping of an extra special quality, which the dealer pompously informed her came from Marlborough College. This we ate with solemn reverence and an awe amounting almost to superstition, though the aristocratic stuff was no better than any other.

Bacon-pudding is a tasty meal, though waning in favour. The old carter may have a fried rasher – without the egg – for breakfast, or fried vegetables, or toasted cheese. Fresh meat is only indulged in once a week, Sundays. That is generally purchased from the van which comes round every Saturday – breast or loin of mutton, or brisket of beef – and is mostly foreign, though some country labourers will not touch the 'furren tackle,' and abhor all tinned goods. At Christmas all the labourers receive a large piece of prime beef, from eight to twelve pounds, and very many a ton of coal at Michaelmas, besides a sum of money. Their drink consists chiefly of tea, very weak – this they have three and very often four times a day – and many keep a small barrel of ale in the house, too, or else fetch it from the inn.

*Alfred Williams*

## GROVELEY, GROVELEY

To the south the downs are crested with the dark coppices of Groveley, the old Royal Chase which gave a tincture of the forest character to all the villages in the valley beneath it. In mediaeval days wild boars abounded there and were the terror of the countryside; there is a legend that Wishford Church was built with the pennies offered in thanksgiving by those who had come safely through the forest. The harsh forest laws prevailed within and around it, but the people on its borders had certain compensating privileges, common pasture for their cattle and pigs in the woods, and the right to pick up wood. Moreover, in the words of a report made in 1603, they 'have an anciente custome and ever tyme out of minde have used to fetch and of right may fetch and bring away bowes at their pleasure from the woods of Groveley from Maie Daie in the morning until Whit Monday at night every Saturday and half hollydaie once, viz., in the evening, and every holledaie and Sabeth daie twice, viz., in the morning and in the evening.' The privileges also included felling and

bringing away, upon 'Holie Thursday (Ascension Day) and upon Whit Monday, one load of trees upon a cart, to be drawn by strength of people.' Also the villagers 'in auntient tyme have used to go in a daunce to the Cathedral Church of our Blessed Ladie in the cittie of New Sarum, on Tuesdaie (in Whitsuntide), and there made their clayme to theire custome in the fforest of Groveley in theis words – 'Groveley, Groveley, and all Groveley.'

These old customs, with their picturesque rites to the accompaniment of the mystic cry of Groveley, Groveley, and all Groveley, are still kept up in a much modified form in Wishford. The ceremonial consists now of gathering live boughs on one day of the year only, and on this hangs the right to pick up dead wood round the whole year in all parts of the forest. At some time the custom got mixed up with the celebration of Oak Apple Day, and now takes place on the 29th of May, instead of Whit-Tuesday. The old procession to Salisbury, six miles away, and the dance round the Cathedral, went on into the eighteenth century, but now the procession is confined to the village, and those who can still dance – they are the old ones – frisk and

CODFORD ST MARY

leap in a green field at home.

Convinced that they would lose their privilege if once they neglected the custom of the 29th of May, the villagers are up at dawn on that day, climbing the rough drove ways and down tracks that lead up to the woods. As early as five o'clock they may be seen returning down the green slopes and streaming into the hollow, looking at a distance like moving trees. Now a single man or woman, walking very fast and seriously, bent beneath the waving green brush of the great bough, with the long stem resting on the shoulder. 'We are bound to do it,' says one, with a sort of solemnity, 'or we could not have the firewood.' Now it is the father of a family, carrying two boughs strung together, and children behind dragging their branches. A gay group of women and girls comes down, all wreathed and mantled in the bright greenery, with hook or hatchet in their hand; foremost steps out a little woman in the cotton hood and sacking apron of the field worker, steadying the great green bough upon her shoulder with one hand, and as she comes near she lifts the other with the hatchet in it, and shrills out the old cry, 'Groveley, Groveley, and all Groveley.' 'There's nothing like it all around,' she explains proudly, "tis Groveley, Groveley, and *all* Groveley, we may go where we like all over the woods.

*Ella Noyes*

## HARVEST HOME

As to the harvest-home, you may easily imagine what a congenial gathering was there; the round, cheery faces, the broad smile, the merry peals of laughter from the maidens, the fogger's ready wit, and old Jemmy's prolonged chuckle. A tremendous fire of logs had been blazing on the wide hearth all the afternoon and evening. The boiler outside had been steaming away, too. The fat hams and beef had been cooking for hours. There was an abundance of vegetables of every kind, and a monster 'roly-poly' plum pudding to crown the board at the finish. The ale stood in great gallon cans; the men drank from large tin cups, the women from glasses. Old Launcelot puffed and blowed like a steam-engine, bringing in the dishes. Jemmy performed the carving, and slivered off the juicy ham and beef.

'Now then, yer, what bist thee gwain to hae, bacon or bif?'

'Aw, gi' I a bit o' that ther 'am, ull ee.'

'Come an, then. Le's hae thi plate yer!' and off he cut the slices of meat, half an inch thick and more.

'Yer, 'old on. Shan't be able to mawv if ee gets that lot down,' the other replied.

'If thee casn't aat that bit thee dossn't want nothin' at aal. I could polish off two or dree sich lots as that. Now, Grubby! jump about a bit, come! Go and get I the steel

HARVEST HOME, LACOCK

Betsy, ull ee? This yer knife dwun cut a bit. Lode a massy! my old ooman's cyarvin' tackle 'ood fetch it off twice as quick. What dost thee want, Smithy? Now, you wenches, clap 'em along yer. No backin' out on't mind; ya got to get it down zomhow.' Here the steel is brought. Skeep, skawp! skeep, skawp! skeep, skawp! 'Tha's better Betsy! Now we shan't be long.' The potatoes and cabbage were piled up; a large brown loaf stood in the middle. No one thought to say grace; all fell to with a will. Jemmy sat at the end of the table with arms sprawled out, and leaned well over, his head almost touching the plate, and shovelled it in, wiping his mouth and mopping his face from time to time with a large red handkerchief.

*Alfred Williams*

## RED OXEN

This afternoon I walked over to Kington St Michael by Langley Burrell Church and Morrell Lane and the old Mausoleum and Langley Ridge and the Plough Inn. It was a day of exceeding and almost unmatched beauty, one of those perfectly lovely afternoons that we seldom get but in September or October. A warm delicious calm and sweet peace brooded breathless over the mellow sunny autumn afternoon and the happy stillness was broken only by the voices of children blackberry gathering in an adjoining meadow and the sweet solitary singing of a robin.

As I drew near Kington I fell in with a team of red oxen, harnessed, coming home from plough with chains rattling and the old ploughman riding the fore ox, reminding me vividly of the time when I used to ride the oxen home from plough at Lanhill.

In spite of the warm afternoon sunshine the solitary cottages, low-lying on the brook, looked cold and damp, but the apples hung bright on the trees in the cottage gardens and a Virginia creeper burned like fire in crimson upon the wall, crimson among the green. When I returned home at night the good Vicar accompanied me as far as the Plough Inn. The moon was at the full. The night was sweet and quiet. Overhead was the vast fleecy sky in which the moon was riding silently and the stillness was

ALDERBURY

broken only by the occasional pattering of an acorn or a chestnut through the leaves to the ground.

*Francis Kilvert*

## LARDY CAKE

The oldest villagers can remember when the Revel was celebrated outside the White Hart. Worthy Vines, who was Gilesman on several occasions, kept the inn then, and had set up there the first village bakery, still maintained by his grandson, George Knapp. Perhaps that was partly why lardy cake had replaced the stubble goose. The lardy, hot and greasy from the oven, is still the Wiltshireman's favourite Saturday tea. It is made of dough left over from the bread-making, rolled out and spread liberally with lard, sugar, well 'plimmed' currants or sultanas and spice – sometimes with candied peel too – and folded over,

spread, and rolled out again and again like flaky pastry. Then it is scored across the top and baked in squarish, well-greased tins, so that when it comes out it looks like a flat mediæval loaf with rounded corners. The perfect lardy is flaked on the top, fatty and rather treacly on the bottom; and between, the shaly layers of rich dough should be neither too close nor too light in texture. It is said that nobody, not even George Knapp, who uses the same recipe, can make lardies as Worthy Vines made them.

*Heather and Robin Tanner*

## FAT PIGS AND HENS

Farmer Chaplin generally thrust his head out of the bedroom window towards eight o'clock, and shouted loudly across the yard for me to have his boots cleaned, or to go and drive the pigs out of the garden, or 'tell Harry to

AVEBURY

put the horse in the trap,' and have it ready by such and such a time. After breakfast, if he did not otherwise go out, he sauntered round, with spotless white shirt, and threw maize about for the poultry, or he might perchance put on a smock and help feed the p8igs, but at best he did not do very much. We used to boil up Indian corn grist in vast quantities for the pigs, and any amount of horse-flesh as well. This seemed a most unnatural thing to me, and I did not like it, but they laughed and said it was 'good stuff, just the sort to make them fat.' Another practice, which I thought most foul and horrible, was to lodge great pieces of raw horse-flesh in the boughs of the apple-trees about the orchard, and let them rot there. This was to provide choice morsels for the hens. The putrefying flesh was soon full of gentils: the hens flocked round, and devoured these with great avidity. People said it 'made them lay well.' Perhaps it did, though I would not have eaten eggs produced from such a diet if I had known anything about it.

We received our wages fortnightly, which was productive of great complaining in my workmate, and then very often master was 'out of cash,' or 'had no change'; sometimes it was a month before we could be settled with. So one day my companion tackled him on the point. 'Sir,' said he, 'do you know how we sort of people live?' The master looked surprised for a moment, and then re-

sponded with, 'N-o! Not hardly.' There are many who do 'not hardly' know how the poor workpeople live. Many there are, too, who do not care; but not all are alike. After this, the master paid us our wages weekly, for he understood then.

*Alfred Williams*

## WINTER WORK

The women do not find much work in the fields during the winter. Now and then comes a day's employment with the threshing-machine when the farmer wants a rick of corn threshed out. In pasture or dairy districts some of them go out into the meadows and spread the manure. They wear gaiters, and sometimes a kind of hood for the head. If done carefully, it is hard work for the arms – knocking the manure into small pieces by striking it with a fork swung to and fro smartly.

In the spring, when the great heaps of roots are opened – having been protected all winter by a layer of straw and earth – it is necessary to trim them before they are used. This is often done by a woman. She has a stool or log of wood to sit on, and arranges a couple of sacks or something of the kind, so as to form a screen and keep off the

SALISBURY PLAIN

bitter winds which are then so common – colder than those of the winter proper. With a screen on one side, the heap of roots the other, and the hedge on the third, she is in some sense sheltered, and, taking her food with her, may stay there the whole day long, quite alone in the solitude of the broad, open, arable fields.

*Richard Jefferies*

## SHEPHERDS

There were Drews and Mintys and Dikes keeping their flocks on the downs when I was a child. In those days they wrapped themselves in great cloaks of navy blue cloth lined with scarlet that their fathers had brought home from the Crimean war – heavy, serviceable, much-treasured cloaks, worn till they fell to pieces. A carter thought his too precious to get wet and would roll it up when rain fell. Occasionally, when these cloaks were offered for sale in Devizes market, a crowd pressed eagerly round to buy them. Cloaks have always been an essential part of a shepherd's dress.

*Ida Gandy*

THE CHRISTMAS TREE for the Sunday Scholars, was quite a new kind of treat for them, as hardly any of them had ever seen one before. It was given yesterday. The tree itself was the gift of Mr Challis, Head Gardener at Wilton and was a fine specimen, standing about 7 or 8 ft from the ground. It was kindly fetched from Wilton by one of Mr Elliott's carts. On its arrival, at about 3 o'clock it was fixed in the class room and was very soon decorated with a large variety of presents of all kinds and sizes, consisting of toys, garments, sweets, dolls etc. Many willing hands made short work and in an hour or two the tree looked like a bit of fairy land. At 6 o'clock refreshments were provided in the way of cake, bread and butter and coffee. After this followed games in which teachers and visitors seemed heartily to join, and at about 7.15 the lamps in the big room were put out and after a few moments of darkness, the door of the classroom was thrown open and the children trooped in to see for themselves the brightly illuminated and decorated tree. There was a hush of admiration, which gave way to louder expressions of satisfaction and merriment, as the children became possessors of the good things displayed before them.

SWINDON RAMBLERS CLUB

COATE RESERVOIR

# Sources & Photographic Details

TEXT

All of the page numbers given below relate to pages in this book, and not the page numbers of the source books.

The main sources for descriptive text are Richard Jefferies and Alfred Williams: Richard Jefferies *Hodge and His Masters* pp. 10, 27, 55, 57, 59, 67, 77, 85, 100, 108 and 120, *Field and Farm* pp. 44 and 63, *Toilers of the Field* pp. 48 and 90, *Chronicles of the Hedges* p. 112, *Field and Hedgrow* pp. 16 and 20; Alfred Williams *A Wiltshire Village* pp. 9, 26, 47, 75, 80, 84, 114, 115, 117 and 119, *Life in a Railway Factory* pp. 32, 33, 35, 68, 70 and 71. Other works used are: W.H. Hudson *A Shepherd's Life* pp. 14, 21 and 87, *A Traveller in Little Things* pp. 22, 79 and 97; A.G. Street *Farmer's Glory* pp. 72, 100, 105 and 111; Geraldine Symons *Children of the Close* pp. 50, 51, 61, and 104; William Plomer (ed.) *Kilvert Diaries* pp. 53, 62, 82 and 118; John Akerman *Akerman's Wiltshire Tales* pp. 12 and 16; Ida Gandy *A Wiltshire Childhood* pp. 94 and 96, *Round About the Little Steeple* pp. 15 and 121; Edward Slow *Wiltshire Rhymes* p. 28; Ella Noyes *Salisbury Plain* pp. 39, 43, 47 and 116; Heather and Robin Tanner *Wiltshire Village* pp. 41, 102, 110 and 119; Rex Sawyer *Bowerchalke Parish Papers* pp. 66 and 76; Mark Girouard *Victorian Country House* p. 83.

Newspapers include The *Devizes and Wiltshire Gazette* pp. 18, 36, 40, 55, 60, 102 and 103; *The Salisbury and Winchester Journal* p. 40; *The Salisbury Times* p. 92; *The Marlborough Times* pp. 106 and 110.

## ILLUSTRATIONS

The credits and information on all the illustrations used in this book are given in page ascending order. Where a source is referred to frequently, only initials are used, and a key to these is at the end of this section. Where dates are known, or can reasonably accurately be deduced, these are given.

Page i half-title, Stralton Sons and Mead's shop in Melksham, *c.* 1900; *WL.* Page ii, Shane's Castle, Devizes, *c.* 1900; *DAB.* Raising stones at Avebury by Steam Power, 1911; *T. Chivers.* Page iii, Children in the market place, Devizes in the 1890s; *DAB.* Page iv, Corsham High Street, 1900; *WL.* Page 1, Pike's Butchers 1911, Market Lavington; *MLM.* Page 2, Minety Cricket Club, *c.* 1900; *WL.* Page 3, Threshing at Ruglands Farm, Avebury, *c.* 1900; *WLS.* Page 4, GWR works seen from the tracks, 1890s; *WL.* Page 5, Two Ladies photographed in a Swindon Street by Mr Harris, a Swindon Cobbler and amateur photographer, *c.* 1900. *Swindon Museum.* Page 6, Mr Hooper with his assistant, outside his studio in Swindon; *WL.* The son of John Chivers, Devizes photographer; *J, Backhouse.* Page 7, Corsham High Street, *c.* 1906; *WL.* Page 8, Selected from a catalogue of Charles Sloper and Son, Devizes, late 1890s; *DAB.* Page 9, East End Farm, Marston, *c.* 1900; *P. Oram.* Page 10, Threshing at Home Farm, Bowood, *c.* 1900; *Trustees of Bowood Collection.* Page 11, Rectory Bridge, Pewsey, *c.* 1900; *RP.* Bratton village, early 1900s; *WL.* Page 12, Enford village, *c.* 1900; *RP.* Isaac Habgood, Bowerchalke, early 1880s; *Rex Sawyer.* Page 13, Easterton village, *c.* 1900; *MLM.* Page 14, Easterton village, *c.* 1900; *MLM.* Page 15, Ox plough team at Calne; *WL.* Page 16, Bat and Ball

Inn, Woodfalls *c.* 1890; *Robert Newman.* Page 17 Job Brown's cottage, Coate, taken by Hooper of Swindon, *c.* 1910; *WL.* Page 18, Potter's Bus in Market Lavington with the Potter family on board, *c.* 1890; *MLM.* Unveiling ceremony of the Estcourt fountain, Devizes, 1879; *Devizes Museum.* Page 19, Devizes Market Place in 1880s; *Devizes Museum.* Page 20, Dressing a carthorse at West Farm, Avebury; *WLS.* Page 21, Silbury Hill; *CPRE.* Page 22, Burbage Road, Pewsey, *c.* 1900; *RP.* Page 23, Fisherton de la Mere and Wylye River, *c.* 1890; *SSWM.* Page 24, The Forge house, Avebury, early 1900s; *WLS.* Page 25, Allington village, nr. Salisbury, *c.* 1900; *SSWM.* Page 26, Pewsey Market Place; *RP.* Page 27, Pewsey Union Workhouse, early 1900s; *RP.* Page 28, Malmesbury Cross decorated for a jubilee celebration, 1887 or 1897; *Pamela Colman.* Page 29, Steeple Ashton High Street, *c.* 1900; *RP.* Henry Jay, Bowerchalke, 1886; *Rex Sawyer.* Page 30, Sutton Veny, *c.* 1900; *WL.* Page 31, Woodman working at Amesbury Park, home of the Antrobus family, 1890s; *SSWM.* Page 32, Branch-line loco, Swindon, 1880s; *WL.* Page 33, GWR factory workers, *c.* 1900; *WL.* Page 34, GWR works, smiths shed; *WL.* Alfred Williams by his hammer at GWR works, *c.* 1910; *Swindon Museum.* Page 35, GWR workers leaving factory, early 1900s; *WL.* Page 36, The KB Stores, Bridge Street, Swindon, *c.* 1900; *WL.* Page 37, Regent Street Swindon, early 1900s; *WL.* Sparkes' Butchers, Regent Street, Swindon, *c.* 1900; *WL.* Page 38, Salisbury Street, Amesbury; *RP.* Page 39, Stonehenge; *CPRE.* Page 40, Perham army camp, North Tidmouth, early 1900s; *WL.* Page 41, Devizes Fire Brigade, 1880s; *DAB.* Page 42, Urchfont village, early 1900s; *Megan Williams.* Ambrose Matthews and his wife in Bratton, *c.* 1900; *WL.* Page 43, Tithe barn, Bradford-on-Avon; *RP.* Shepherd Jacob Sound, Cheverell; *WL.* Page 44, Sheep Shearers at Berwick Bassett, 1890s; *WLS.* Page 45, Aldbourne in floods, *c.* 1900; *Michael Palmer.* Woodborough village, *c.* 1900; *RP.* Page 46, Fisherton de lat Mere, 1890s; *SSWM.* Imber, grocer's shop and Forge cottage *c.* 1900; *SSWM.* Page 47, Imber, early 1900s; *SSWM.* Page 48, Steam threshing at Market Lavington; *MLM.* Page 49, Hayrick building nr. Avebury, *c.* 1900; *WLS.* Mill Street, Trowbridge, 1903; *WL.* Page 50, Mrs Willcox and friend, Warminster, *c.* 1910; *WM.* Page 51, The Poultry Cross, Salisbury, *c.* 1900; *WL.* Page 52, Willcox family, owners of the Warminster Motor Company, at tea, *c.* 1910; *WM.* Salisbury Close gate, *c.* 1900; *WL.* Page 53, Vicarage, Kington St Michael, Mrs Synge with the children; *WL.* Page 54, Amesbury Church, 1880s; *SSWM.* Page 55, Devizes Cycling Club at Stonehenge, 1895; *Lionel Hailstone.* Page 56, The Green, Marlborough, early 1900s; *WM.* Page 57, Fisherton de la Mere, 1890s; *SSWM.* Page 58, Kitchen dresser and maid a Lacock Abbey, *c.* 1870; *FTM.* Page 59, Waggon and Horses at Beckhampton, before 1900; *WLS.* Page 60, Electric bus at Melksham; *WL.* Bear and Castle Hotel, Marlborough, *c.* 1900; *RP.* Page 61, The Kemm family at Avebury Manor; *WLS.* The youngest member of the Pratt family, Avebury; *WLS.* Page 62, Sunday School tea at Collett's vicarage, Bowerchalke; *Rex Sawyer.* Page 63, Avebury School group, *c.* 1900; *WLS.* Page 64, Market day in Calne, *c.* 1900; *WL.* Page 65, Estate staff at Bowood, nr. Calne, *c.* 1900; *Trustees of the Bowood Collection.* T.H. White, agricultural engineers, Market Lavington, *c.* 1900; *MLM.* Page 66, Marlborough High Street; *WL.* Page 67, Salisbury Market Place; *SSWM.* Page 68, Warminster, *c.* 1900; *WM.* Page 69, GWR works dining room, Swindon; *WL.* Purton village; *Swindon Museum.* Page 70, Regent Circus, Swindon, *c.* 1900; *WL.* Page 71, Boarding trains on Trip Day, Swindon, early 1900s; *Swindon Museum.* Trip Day postcard, one of a series; *Swindon Museum.* Page 72, GWR Children's Fête; *Swindon Society.* Page 73, Ludgershall, Butt Street; *RP.* Page 74, Wroughton; *Swindon Museum.* Page 75, Fisherton de la Mere Church,

1890s; *SSWM*. Page 76, Warminster Market Place; *WM*. The Carrier's Cart, Bowerchalke, 1884; *Rex Sawyer*. Page 77, Salisbury Market; *RP*. Page 78, Church Walk, Trowbridge; *RP*. Page 79, Cricklade cattle market, 1890s; *Swindon Museum*. Page 80, Blacklands Mill, Calne, 1890s; *WL*. Page 81, Highworth; *WL*. Page 82, Edington Church, 1890s; *SSWM*. Lord and Lady Lansdowne at Bowood House, nr. Calne, 1890s; *Trustees of the Bowood Collection*. Page 83, Spye Park, Bowden Hill, 1870s; *Michael Grey*. Page 84, Westbury White Horse and sheep fold, 1890s; *RP*. Page 85, Milking team; *RP*. Page 86, Porch House, Potterne, *c*. 1905; *WL*. Page 87, Gastard village nr. Corsham, *c*. 1905; *WL*. Page 88, Hunt meet at the George and Dragon, Rowde; *Tim and Helen Withers*. Page 89, High Street and Town Bridge, Chippenham, *c*. 1900; *Devizes Museum*. Tom Haines and his family, Market Lavington's last town crier; *MLM*. Page 90, Haymaking at Bowerchalke, 1885; *Rex Sawyer*. Page 91, Harvesting at Bowerchalke, 1890; *Rex Sawyer*. Page 92, Truffle hunting at Winterslow, 1910; *Hulton Picture Library*. Mr Yeates and his truffle dogs, 1910; *SSWM*. Page 93, High Street, Ramsbury, *c*. 1900; *RP*. Boys haymaking at Marston school; *P. Oram*. Page 94, Bishops Cannings; *A. Alexander*. Page 95, Boy on his way to Aldbourne carnival, 1890s; *WLS*. Page 96, Peapickers at Little Cheverell, *c*. 1900; *WL*. Bishop's Cannings Church; *A. Alexander*. Page 97, Aldbourne Band; *M. Palmer*. Page 98, Chitterne village; *A. Alexander*. Page 99, Seend Church, 1890s; *WL*. Page 100, Sail reaper nr. Avebury, 1880s; *WLS*. Page 101, Steam threshing at Winterborne Monckton; *WLS*. Page 102, Avebury Stone circle, 1890s; *WL*. Page 103, Amesbury people protesting at the first enclosure and charges at Stonehenge, 1901; *WL*. Page 104, Salisbury fair, *c*. 1900; *WL*. Page 105, William Taylor's famous fairground attraction, early 1900s; *Jennings family*. Page 106, The Rink, Swindon, *Dennis Bird*. Page 107, Mop Fair at Marlborough, early 1900s; *Devizes Museum*. William Taylor's girls who danced to attract the crowds to his shows, early 1900s; *Jennings Family*. Page 108, Ploughboy of seventeen years, Avebury; *WLS*. Cottagers from Heytesbury; *WL*. Page 109, Drove Road, Swindon, *c*. 1890; *WL*. Page 110, The smithy at Figheldean; *RP*. Page 111, Barne's Shop in Calne, 1890s; *WL*. Page 112, Spotted Cow Inn, Coate nr. Swindon; *Dennis Bird*. Page 113, Wilton; *WL*. Police house, Bishopstone; *RP*. Page 114, Manor Cottages, Avebury; *WLS*. Page 115, Gypsy family and caravan; *WM*. Page 116, Oak-apple Day celebrations at Great Wishford, 1906; *A. Moulding*. Page 117, Codford St Mary; *WM*. Page 118, Harvest home celebrations at Lacock, 1870s; *FTM*. Page 119, Alderbury postoffice, 1890s; *SSWM*. Page 120, Wedding at Avebury, 1890s; *WLS*. Page 121, Shepherd on Salisbury Plain; *SSWM*. Page 122, Swindon Ramblers Cycle Club, 1890s; *WL*. Coate reservoir; *WL*.

*Key:* DAB, David Buxton, author collection. MLM, Market Lavington Museum. WLS, Wiltshire Life Society. WL, Wiltshire Library and Museum Service. SSWM, Salisbury and South Wilts Museum. WM, Warminster Museum. FTM, Fox Talbot Museum. RP, Roger Pope.

A